THE
WATER
WILL
HOLD YOU

THE
WATER
WILL
HOLD YOU

*A Skeptic Learns
to Pray*

Lindsey Crittenden

HARMONY BOOKS
NEW YORK

Author's Note: This book is a memoir. The events narrated herein all happened and are recounted as I remember them. Some incidents have been conflated for expediency's sake, and some names have been changed. Any errors are my own.

HARMONY BOOKS is a registered trademark and the Harmony Books colophon is a
trademark of Random House, Inc.

Portions of this book have been published, in slightly different form, in the following
publications: *Real Simple, Reader's Digest, Santa Monica Review, Health, Image,* and *Best
American Spiritual Writing 2004.* The author gratefully acknowledges these publications.

Grateful acknowledgment is made to the Division of Christian Education of the
National Council of the Churches of Christ for permission to use, except where noted,
the Scripture quotations from the New Revised Standard Version Bible, copyright
© 1989 by the Division of Christian Education of the National Council of the churches
of Christ in the United States of America. Used by permission. All rights reserved.

All psalms and liturgical quotations are taken from the Book of Common Prayer of the
Episcopal Church USA, 1979.

Library of Congress Cataloging-in-Publication Data
Crittenden, Lindsey,
The water will hold you: a skeptic learns to pray / Lindsey Crittenden.—1st ed.
1. Crittenden, Lindsey. 2. Spiritual biography. 3. Spiritual life. 4. Prayer—
Christianity. 5. Spiritual healing. I. Title.
BR1725.C745A3 2007
248.092--dc22
[B]   2006026005

ISBN 978-0-307-34735-0

Printed in the United States of America

Design by Lauren Dong

10 9 8 7 6 5 4 3 2 1

First Edition

For Claire Elizabeth Pflueger Blake, my godmother,
and Clare Elizabeth McCarthy, my goddaughter

So that in seeking you, we might find you.
BOOK OF COMMON PRAYER, EUCHARIST PRAYER D

Il n'y a pas de moyen de faire le premier pas; il faut le faire.

PROLOGUE

I jumped in the first time when I was eight.

It was a hot day in the East Bay suburbs, on the other side of the tunnel from the San Francisco fog. Fathers jiggled tall glasses in which ice cubes rattled, while mothers dangled their bare legs in the shallow end and called to the children to "Slow down," "No running," and "Stop teasing." My three-year-old brother, strapped into a squishy rubber contraption, bobbed like a cork in the shallow end.

"Look!" I called out, my toes curled over the end of the diving board.

My mother shielded her eyes with a flattened hand. My father stood in a cluster of chuckling men. Mom always watched, so getting Dad's attention mattered more.

"Look, Daddy!"

He did.

Now.

I looked down. Water: familiar, hospitable, heated to a comfortable eighty-four degrees. I'd been in it all afternoon. And yet, it looked different from up here: foreign, discrete. Sure, it was contained in the kidney-shaped concrete of a suburban backyard, but still.

I looked up again. Daddy and the other men were still watching. I bit my lip, snapped my bathing suit over a slice of buttock.

"Go ahead," my mother called. "We're watching."

My toes rubbed against one another.

"The water will hold you," my swimming teacher had said. I had been four and learning to float by standing in the shallow end and leaning back. When my hands and feet scrambled in alarm, the water acted like water—liquid, as penetrable as air. But when I relaxed, as I gradually did, with Mrs. Ursula just a few inches away, the water didn't give. I'd had to learn how, and once I had, I'd never forgotten.

I stepped back to the edge, looked down. The object of my longing lay before me, intact. Floating with my face just beneath the water, I'd looked up through its surface so many times, enthralled to be *in* what I was now looking down on. The surface was just that, a surface; what lay beneath was something else, another realm entirely. I bent my knees.

"*Daddy!* Look!"

He rattled his glass. "Tell you what," he called out. "Let me know just before you hit the water, okay?"

"Jim!": my mother, half chiding, half humored.

Next thing I knew, I'd plunged through, breaking the surface. I'd carried water in a bucket when Dad washed the car. I knew it was heavy. And yet my body cut it like a knife. I'd broken that mesmerizing membrane, that scrim between air and underwater. I was in. Water slid against my skin, my suit pulled up like a wedgie, water forced up my nose. I couldn't grab hold but I didn't need to. It held me.

CHAPTER ONE

Prayer changed my life.

But first I had to start praying.

One Sunday in 1996, I walked into All Souls Episcopal Church. I didn't know what I believed. I didn't know *if* I believed. I just knew I felt worse than I'd known I could feel. I'd woken at four A.M., the way I'd been waking for months, to stumble down the hall as my stomach twisted in knots, and then to get back in bed and pull the covers over my head. I dreaded the light that pressed against the windows. All I had to do that day was laundry and paper grading, and it felt unbearable. At dawn, the squirrels who lived in the crawl space overhead began to tumble and cavort. I pulled the pillow over my head. No good. My mind was awake, and it wasn't letting go.

The clock ticked toward 7:30. And then, at 7:50, I got up. I kicked back the covers, stepped onto the rug that never felt quite clean no matter how frequently I vacuumed, and pulled on jeans and a turtleneck. I swished water around in my mouth and ran a comb through my hair. I grabbed my coat, stepped out of the apartment, and locked the door behind me. Within three minutes, I was there.

I passed All Souls every day, admiring its neatly tended bed of cyclamen and the simple sign announcing Hours of Worship. I considered its A-frame architecture part of my new neighborhood's landscape, no more significant than the blowsy pine tree in front of my building or the yellow house at the corner. I hadn't met many people or made any new friends in North Berkeley, but I'd become familiar with the terrain of overgrown gardens and jasmine-tangled fences between Black Oak Books, Peet's Coffee, and my apartment. I'd moved in during August; on October 1, I thought, *It's my favorite month of the year. I'll shake this funk off any day now.* Now it was early December, and I felt as anxious as ever. SUNDAY EUCHARIST AT 8 AND 10, the tasteful lettering read.

I looked for a back door to sneak in without having strangers press me with questions or quizzical smiles. No such luck. A tall, pale man stood inside the open double doors, and he'd seen me. In his blue suit and tie, his neatly combed damp hair, he seemed a proper parish representative, someone with whom I'd have little in common. He handed me a bulletin. I stepped inside. The light was still pale at eight o'clock, as the earth tilted toward the winter solstice, and I sat at the end of a pew near a narrow window. I pulled my sleeves down around my fists and tucked them under my crossed arms. Someone up front—an older woman, in neatly coiffed hair and a dress—cleared her throat, and the room felt incipient with a different kind of quiet from the ricocheting isolation I was used to at home. This quiet breathed nervousness, yes—but also expectation and potential.

My stomach grumbled and churned, and I clenched my hands. They felt so small, the bones moving against each other in the pressure of my grasp. Maybe I should leave, go buy the *New York Times,* sit at Katz's over a plate of eggs like a normal person on a Sunday morning. I took another look around: I was the only person under fifty. And then a man moved into the pew in front of me, and I felt relief at his youth. He wore a suit, too, its fabric reminding me of the down parkas, popular in seventh grade, that appeared black in most lighting but, outside, could take on the shimmer of beetle green. He glanced at me with large, moist dark eyes behind oversized, thick lenses, and I looked away. Where had he and the pale man and the coiffed woman come from? I never saw such attire on the streets of Berkeley. He pulled out a rosary and began to click through its beads, and my eyes widened in alarm. Wasn't this an Episcopal church? Weren't rosaries a Catholic thing, a hocus-pocus accoutrement, like a fully detailed crucifix over an iron bed in every movie ever made about Italian-Americans?

My doubts went inward. Would something in my stance or casual attire give me away as a lapsed Episcopalian, a doubter? I knew I couldn't take communion: It would be disrespectful and dishonest, since I didn't believe in all that it was supposed to mean. I'd left my wallet at home, I realized; I couldn't even put money in the plate.

I could leave, but I'd have to pass that tall pale man again. And besides, sitting in this space, quiet with the breathing of strangers, felt good. Better than being at home with the laundry and my anxiety. The church's bare wooden walls and innocuous beige carpeting and simple altar felt surprisingly reassuring, even with the oversized pastel banner quilted with a cross. A few more people arrived, although most pews remained empty, and when I turned around I saw the tall pale man lined up with another usher and two priests, and they all began walking down the center aisle. I stood along with everyone else in the congregation. Behind the procession, beneath the mezzanine-level choir (which was empty; eight A.M. service, I'd later learn, was said, not sung), lettering proclaimed ALL SOULS ARE MINE, SAITH THE LORD.

What was I doing there, anyway?

If asked, I might have said I was new to the neighborhood and looking to meet people. I might have told how I'd gone to college in Berkeley, twelve years earlier, but how my friends from those days were married or had moved away. I had family nearby in San Francisco—my parents and six-year-old nephew—but I hadn't found the sense of belonging that I'd thought returning to my native Bay Area would bring. I missed New York, where I'd lived for nine years before returning to California for grad school. Now I was struggling with shaping a life as a freelance writer and editor and part-time teacher after the security of a master's program and, before that, a full-time job.

I'm here, I imagined saying, *doing research.* I'd recently written a piece on East Bay swimming pools for a local paper; maybe I'd do similar reconnaissance on Berkeley houses of worship. I'd considered visiting the synagogue down the street, the Presbyterian parish up the hill, the boxy Society of Friends building a mile away. I'd been raised Episcopalian, I could have mentioned—but the fact of my upbringing held no allegiance beyond the fact that here, I thought as I watched the procession, I knew what to do.

I'm here because I need somewhere to go, I thought as I watched the priest bow low before the altar and then turn to face the congregation, her arms outstretched—but I couldn't imagine saying it. I couldn't imagine telling the truth of what had brought me to All Souls that December day, because I couldn't admit it to myself.

Spiritual longing was not in my vocabulary. I had nothing against religion per se; we went to St. Stephen's Episcopal Church every Sunday of my childhood. I'd helped my mother prepare for the Sunday school classes she taught one year, scooping nut meat out of walnut halves to place a pulled-apart cotton ball and a tiny plastic baby inside and glue with a strap of gold cord, as Christmas ornaments for the kindergarteners. I'd attended youth group in seventh and eighth grades. Then our priest went through a divorce and my parents sided with his wife. Youth group lost its appeal after Julie Bassett announced to everyone on a summer retreat that I'd gotten my period. In high school and college, I set foot in churches only for a wedding or a funeral. I'd gone to Easter services a few times during my years in New York, sitting in the back in various Greenwich Village parishes and considering myself superior to the people in their frilly dresses and huge pink and yellow hats; we were all there because it was Easter, I knew, just as we'd all show up on Christmas Eve, too. At least I didn't pretend to be a faithful regular by taking communion.

My first Easter in New York, I'd walked home past a glorious tulip magnolia just in bloom. *That's my religion,* I thought as I relished the feeling of sunshine on my bare legs after my first East Coast winter. I was willing to consider the existence of a divine deity, but I could not imagine putting aside my rational mind, my doubts, to swallow the more far-fetched tenets of religion. Not to mention all the horrors done in religion's (or God's) name. Church might provide a quiet place on a Sunday morning, a way of meeting neighbors. I didn't think beyond that.

And then the congregation spoke. *"We believe in one holy and Catholic church."*

We do?

There was more.

"Only son of God."

"Born of a virgin."

"Died and rose again."

No surprise, really—after all, I was in *church.* But I couldn't imagine suspending my critical faculties to swallow those amazing claims. Nor could I imagine wanting to. My stomach churned.

This isn't for me.

But I stayed. I didn't take communion. I wasn't going to partake in something I didn't believe in. My fingers worked one another like beads. I crossed and uncrossed my legs, rested my shoes against the kneeling rail and then heard my mother's voice telling me not to put my feet on the furniture. During the Peace, I shook the hands of the people around me and let myself be stiffly embraced by an older woman who called me "dear." During the passing of a polished-brass collection plate, I stared at my lap and pretended to have found a fascinating spot on the knee of my jeans.

During the sermon, I wept.

The priest, a pleasant-looking woman with cardboard-colored hair and rose-tinted glasses, started by talking about *call,* a strong inner prompting, often interpreted as divine vocation. She mentioned Moses and Abraham and Joseph, and then cited secular, real-life examples, enumerating the inherent risk and opportunity for connection in following a hunch, in taking a chance. I thought of moving to New York City when I was twenty-two and knew only three people there; I thought of coming back to California for grad school; I thought of writing. I felt my hands unclench, and I listened as intently as I had a week earlier at a reading at Black Oak Books.

"I'd like to read from Rilke now," the priest said.

Rilke? I sat up straight, stretched my neck to see her open what looked like a well-worn volume. I felt chastised for my earlier, uncharitable thoughts about the hokey banner. The poem, called "The Annunciation," fit the gospel reading since that morning was the first Sunday in Advent, although I didn't know that yet.

"He looked," the priest read, from Rilke's description of the appearance of the angel Gabriel to the teenaged Mary, *"and she looked up at him, their looks so merged in one . . ."*

Every pore in my body seemed to open, every word to chip away at something inside me. *"The world outside grew vacant suddenly, and all things being seen, endured and done, were crowded into them."* I thought of my therapist's office, of moments with friends and lovers when I felt most intensely the struggle to open up, to be seen. I thought of my brother. As the priest finished the poem—*"Just she and he—see, this arouses fear"*—tears ran down my cheeks. The poem had stunned me.

At the conclusion of the service, the congregation followed the altar party down the aisle. The priest stood in a receiving line just beneath ALL SOULS ARE MINE, SAITH THE LORD. I rehearsed a two-line introduction and, as my turn came to shake her hand, readied my face into a bland expression as I said my name and that I lived up the street.

"I'm Pamela Cranston," the priest responded with a smile, her blue eyes keen. "Are you new to the neighborhood?"

"A few months."

"A student?" she asked, a logical question given our proximity to the UC campus.

"No," I said. "I'm a writer."

She nodded. "Berkeley has a lot of writers. I'm one too." She gave a little chuckle, one that felt more inclusive than dismissive. "We should talk. I'm in every Wednesday afternoon. Come see me." Other congregants waited for their turn; I could sense their breathing behind me. I gave a quick smile and said, "Okay."

TEN DAYS LATER, walking again down Cedar Street to All Souls, I wondered what Pamela and I would talk about. Yes, I'd been moved by her sermon, but loving Rilke was such a cliché, as though I were still clutching my pink-highlighted paperback of *Letters to a Young Poet.* I was reminded of college in more ways than one: I'd never attended office hours because I never had a specific enough question for the professor or TA.

I'd always been good with authority figures, but I didn't always know how to bridge the gap of formality with them. My father had seared my young consciousness when, in fourth grade, I brought home a C in math and he told me, "There's no excuse for carelessness." I'd spent the following twenty-six years being careful, but I didn't always know how to be myself.

And she was a *priest.* She might see through me to the anxious woman, the skeptic, the little girl who'd once blown spit bubbles in church and raised her hand in Sunday school to say that Christ was Jesus' last name. Church meant patent-leather Mary Janes, which I swung from the hard, wooden pew until my mother's hand pressed on my legs to quiet them. It meant my father growing restless during the liturgy and sermons, as he grew restless everywhere except the garden and the kitchen. It meant watching him take my squirming brother by the hand as an excuse to go outside, where Mom and I found them after the service—Blake climbing a tree, Dad smoking and chatting with the senior warden. It meant learning how to blow raspberries on my arm in Sunday school, and it meant youth group humiliation. Around the time we stopped attending St. Stephen's, my mother started saying things like "God is in nature" and "Organized religion is full of hypocrites." Even Dad—such a stickler for detail that he once jabbed the Rite of Marriage page in the Book of Common Prayer during a wordy wedding homily, stage-whispering, "It's all right here, good enough for the kings of England"—would look sage and offer only that "Faith is a personal thing."

And, above all, church meant doubt: doubt about belief, doubt about how to package myself, doubt about what I was doing walking through the basement doorway of All Souls. Admitting anxiety felt contrary not only to the way I'd been raised but to my instinct. I didn't want pity, especially from someone who might foist God on me. And I certainly wasn't looking for God, I reminded myself as I tapped on a door.

Pamela opened it with a smile.

"Welcome." She took my hand in both of hers. "Come in." She gestured me toward a low chair near a wall of overflowing bookshelves and sat down in a swivel chair next to a desk, crossing plump legs beneath a denim wraparound skirt. With her floral blouse, brown pumps, and twinkling eyes, she reminded me of a librarian in a British mystery.

"So," she said, "tell me what brings you to All Souls."

The upholstery of the chair felt scratchy as I heard myself repeat the line about being new to the neighborhood, about wanting to meet people. "I'm not sure I'm ready to attend church," I admitted. "I'm not sure what I believe."

She nodded. "One of the great things about the Anglican church is its acceptance of questions."

Had I made a mistake, wandered into a splinter cult? I remembered the rosary of the man in front of me the previous Sunday. "I thought this was an Episcopal church."

"Episcopalianism is the American branch of the Anglican Communion, which has its seat in the Church of England."

"Oh," I said. "Henry the Eighth and his divorce."

"Yes, in part." She sighed as though she'd been over this many times. "There's a lot more to our church than one king's battle with the Pope." She cited several books that provided a helpful summary of church history, and I dutifully wrote their titles on a notepad. I was on familiar terrain, taking notes, asking scholarly questions, even as I doubted I'd ever set foot in the theological union bookstore to which she gave detailed directions.

I told her I'd been baptized Episcopalian. She told me she'd been a nun—another discovery for me; I'd thought nuns an exclusively Roman Catholic enterprise—and we shared memories of Grace Cathedral in candlelight. "I did youth group in junior high," I said, shifting again against the upholstery. She nodded politely. "My mom taught Sunday school. My dad was on the vestry." Was I trying to impress her? Or was I just searching for common ground?

The room ticked with silence. Glancing around, I observed photographs, framed icons, more books, a small cross on the wall. A window opened onto a parking lot, which All Souls shared with the apartment building next door. It wasn't much of a view— a Cyclone fence, the tops of trees—and yet Pamela's office felt cozy, conducive to work and to quiet, productive thinking—the antithesis of what I'd been encountering at home. My mind went blank as I searched for more facts to dredge up, more comments to bridge the silence.

"I'm looking to meet more people." My mouth was dry, and the words felt like marbles. That reason, I knew as soon as I spoke it, wasn't even a minor factor in what had brought me to All Souls, but I kept talking. "Especially single people. Men."

"Let me think," she said, and I turned the page in my notebook, pen poised. "We don't have too many single folks. There's Jerry, who's going through a divorce. Very painful time for him. Saint Mark's, on campus, has more single people." But I'd already given up at her use of the word *folks.*

"I haven't been with anyone for a while," I admitted, thinking of my last relationship, if I could even call it that—a fling with a grad student. "If ever. I mean a real relationship." I'd been covering this territory in therapy, and I heard myself articulating some of the phrases my therapist had offered up, phrases I'd resisted from the couch but now parroted back. "I haven't always been straightforward about what I want. I have a hard time trusting."

"Yes," Pamela said. "Trust is tough."

My eyes returned again to the icon above her desk, next to the cross. Mary, I assumed—the Virgin or Magdalene, I wasn't sure which. Her large black eyes seemed to mirror an endless patience, a willingness to wait and see that I couldn't imagine feeling. There was something else, too, something I *could* relate to: an unstaunchable sadness.

"I lost my brother."

She sucked in her breath, and I continued. "He died—was shot, actually . . ."

"I'm so sorry to hear that. When?"

"Almost three years ago. January eighth, 1994."

"Oh. So you're working through the acceptance."

She must have read something in my face, because she quickly added, "Not that it happens in four neat stages. I lost my brother, too. Also at Christmastime. Christmas Eve, in fact. It ruined Christmas for me."

"We went out of town the first year over the holidays, so as not to be home."

"Smart move. How old was he?"

"Twenty-six."

"Older or younger?"

"Younger. Five years."

She sighed. "The world doesn't always recognize that pain, does it? There's a lot of attention to the parents, the spouse, the children. But siblings are often overlooked."

Staring at the floor, my eyes filled. We'd found common ground. And yet what did all this have to do with church?

"Death's a bitch, isn't it?"

Surprised, I looked up and met her gaze. I knew then that I wasn't going to get a catechism drill on Life Eternal or a request to sign on the dotted line of a Returning to the Fold form.

"Yes," I said.

She asked about my writing and said she was working on

a mystery novel. I told her I'd worked at St. Martin's Press, a publisher of many mysteries, and gave her suggestions about submitting queries. I no longer noticed the upholstery.

"You're lucky," I said. "You have this office." Its space was feeling more and more appealing, and in it I could imagine not only focus but a kind of intellectual approach to spirituality that I had never considered. There were crosses and prayer books and icons, yes; but there also were tomes of poetry and analysis and thought. There was no sign of squirrels or unpaid bills. I told Pamela about my job teaching high school English, as well as the freelance editing I was starting to do. And then I heard myself say, "I've been struggling a little."

"Grief," Pamela said, "takes a long time to work through."

"It's more than grief," I said, although I didn't know what to call it. *Depression* seemed such an attention-getting word, such an exaggeration—even as I battled its symptoms and filled out its diagnosis code on my Blue Cross claims. I knew how it felt, the constant undermining that manifested itself in agitation and dry heaves, lack of appetite and a sense of tension so pitched I sometimes thought my fingers would snap off when I rubbed them together. Indeed, alone with my journal or sitting with my therapist or a close friend, trying to explain how I felt just made me feel worse. "What do you think triggered this?" friends would ask, and the pit in my stomach would seem a bowling ball. I thought of my mother's familiar retort: "I just don't understand," as though I were holding something back from her. "You're living where you wanted to live, you have the apartment you wanted, you have the teaching job you wanted, you're writing. Everything is going just as you wanted!"

I didn't get it, either.

Friends offered advice. Go on meds; hang out at a bar; volunteer at a soup kitchen; find a fun, clean man for noncommittal sex. None of these options appealed. Not long before my visit to All Souls, a friend had presented me with a slip of paper on which she'd written the name of a psychiatric clinic at Stanford. Her concern had touched me, before it made me feel worse. Was I that bad off? I preferred the stance of another college friend, who listened patiently one morning when I asked if she'd drive me to an appointment because I felt too scared to get on the freeway, and then said, "I think it's something you need to do for yourself. You can, you know."

Sometimes, in my search for an answer, I latched onto one definable factor as the key, usually while listening to a public radio interview on melancholy or glancing at a women's magazine cover headline about learned optimism. I'd feel a brief flare of relief, usually followed by an hour of manic list-making on what I could do to fix the problem, until I woke the following morning to find the list totally beside the point.

Pamela's attribution of grief felt like one such graspable reason, but her predictable implication made me impatient. Hadn't I already spent close to three years "working through" grief? Didn't I already know the extent of pain I'd felt over losing my brother, pain that had—one morning six months after his death, as I bent to pick up my newspaper from a square of sunlight outside my front door—made me wonder how I could continue to live? If I'd learned anything in the previous two years, I'd learned about grief, and I knew that, as huge a part as my brother had played in my life, my anxiety had its source elsewhere.

"I'm doing what I want to do," I told Pamela, "but . . ."

I heard my therapist's voice: "You're taking a risk," Dr. B.

would say, or, with heavy irony, "Oh, I see. Commitment is supposed to come anxiety free." Everyone said I was too hard on myself.

Again, Pamela seemed to follow my thoughts. "Do you have a therapist to talk to?"

I nodded, gave a rueful smile. "Twice a week."

"She must be good."

"He. I saw a woman in New York, but now, well, I like him and I've had a hard time getting close to men, partly because of my brother, so it's helping."

She nodded.

"I just don't know how much longer . . ."

This, too, was a familiar refrain: Was I such a self-indulgent mess I'd be in therapy forever? I'd already clocked three years in New York; now I was well into my third year with Dr. B. I'd had my first appointment with him two days after Blake died, although I'd made the appointment weeks beforehand. We spent the first six months talking about the loss before we got around to what had brought me in the first place.

"It takes what it takes," Pamela said. "Depression is a disease. It's nothing to feel responsible for, you know. You have a lot on your plate."

I nodded. Hearing her use the word *depression* demystified some of its taboo. I blamed myself for not being able to pull myself out of the black hole, for not being resilient or strong enough, and when someone acknowledged what I was up against, I often felt defensive. Today, I blinked back tears. Pamela had given me a kind of permission.

"You know," and she gave a wry smile, "we find God at the end of our ropes."

Her tone hadn't changed, but the tweed of the chair suddenly scratched more than ever. The silence ticked. Mary's eyes shone opaquely from the icon.

"But I'm a mess," I said. "I feel awful. I feel like shit."

"God doesn't mind." Her face looked calm and assured, not at all smug or preachy. "Have you tried prayer?"

It would be rude to get up now. And yet, as much as I bristled with discomfort, a quiet voice said, *Stay. Hear her out.*

As a child, I'd learned "Now I lay me down to sleep, I pray the Lord my soul to keep, If I should die before I wake, I pray the Lord my soul to take." The mention of death had confused me: Was it that easy to slip away? My mother soothed me—of course I wouldn't die that night or anytime soon—but I lay awake wondering why, then, the prayer included such an option. As far as the Lord's Prayer, its petition to "forgive us our trespasses, as we forgive those who trespass against us" made me think only of the NO TRESPASSING sign in the backyard of the house I took a shortcut through on the way home from school. Those childhood prayers fell far short.

"I don't know how."

"Yes, you do," Pamela said. "You just admitted you feel like shit. That's a start."

My eyes filled again. I'd been crying out "Help" in the car and underwater in the swimming pool, where no one could hear. Desperation that blatant and raw felt embarrassing but oddly liberating and justified, too. But didn't supplication need an outside audience, the way I'd been teaching my students that effective persuasive argument did? In fact, wasn't prayer just another word for persuasive argument?

As a child at St. Stephen's, I didn't understand what *messiah* meant or how Jesus could be a baby in a manger, a carpenter, the Son of God, and the Risen Lord at the same time. But I did understand that prayer was private, a grown-up thing. When the priest was done and the songs were over and we'd gone for our little flat wafer (I associated the word *host* with bags of favors and Musical Chairs), the grown-ups would assemble themselves into what seemed mostly a question of posture: hands clasped, eyes closed, back straight. My father genuflected, the only one in our 1960s Low Church parish to do so. My mother didn't press her flat palms together (the way she'd taught me to do) as much as lower her entire face into her open hands, as though to disappear. Where did she go? In her wool suit, her pumps, her pantyhose, she was still recognizably Mommy—but she became Other, too. Pure self. Sitting next to her, I first realized she had a life of her own, an identity beyond that of mother and wife. I felt awed and had to hold back the urge to reach out my finger and poke her, gently: "Mommy? You there?"

And then when I was ten and my cat was hit by a car, I discovered that prayer is born of need. "Please God, let Burmaspring Elizabeth live. I'll do anything you want," I begged every night into my Wizard of Oz pillowcase, which I always turned over so I didn't have to rest my cheek against the Wicked Witch. That was my first honest prayer. When my cat returned home with one cloudy blind eye and a wired jaw, though, I had no idea how to live up to it.

I still didn't.

"I don't even know if I believe," I told Pamela. Eucalyptus branches swayed on the other side of the window and, when a car backfired in the parking lot, she appeared not to hear.

"God doesn't mind."

Her words went counter to the good posture I'd mimicked, the demeanor I'd always associated with belief. St. Stephen's had not been a finger-wagging church, and I couldn't recall any parental or priestly message that God was mean or vengeful. I'd been raised on a God of love and compassion. And yet I held the conviction that God was the ultimate grown-up and I'd better be on my best behavior—even if I wasn't sure God existed. *For the sake of argument,* I thought as I searched Pamela's face for a glimpse of irony and found none, *let's suppose God is real. Well, then he's an authority figure and as such he would spot carelessness. Or at least he should.*

"Doesn't God have any self-respect?" I asked.

"Nope." Pamela grinned. "God's not proud. He's just happy to see you."

In a nightmare I had frequently as a child, I found myself naked in the middle of Bayview Avenue (where we lived until I was six) in broad daylight. My parents walked with me, and as I scurried to the curb to hide behind the big-finned cars, they told me not to be silly. "Come on," they told me. "Nobody's looking." Exposure made me feel like hiding, even with people I knew and trusted. That's what I was working on with my therapist, and that's what had made me cry during Pamela's sermon: Rilke's recognition of the intimacy—the fear—of being seen, of opening up, and of doing it anyway.

I yearned for that release. I was crying for help in the swimming pool and begging friends to drive me to my appointments, after all. I couldn't have it both ways.

Pamela was knocking down my objections, one after another. I kept coming up with more.

Surely, if prayer didn't depend upon belief or posture, it still demanded the right words. Ad-libbing wouldn't work. I was working every morning on short stories and writing for a local newspaper, but I was also filling my journal and a computer file called "Ycch" with circular rambles that took me nowhere. Once my guide through any labyrinth, words had become either the reverberation of an anxious mind or a dictatorial imperative to figure myself out. Neither seemed a way to relief—or belief. I loved wrestling a long sentence into parallel syntax, loved sprinkling order onto my ideas with a semicolon here, a dash there. I loved losing myself in a world of my own divining; when the work went well, everything made sense at the keyboard, but the freedom and thrill I'd discovered as a girl of eight, sitting up in bed with a notebook propped against my knees and cinnamon toast crumbs on my fingers, now resisted me. I often jabbed out a series of letters that made no sense or stabbed a page with my pen.

"I wouldn't know what to say," I told Pamela.

"The Prayer Book has many good prayers." She'd already explained the various editions of the Book of Common Prayer, a staple in every Episcopal pew and representations of which sat just above my elbow on her bookshelves. "'Help' is a good start. You might try '*God you are here, God I am here.*' Or the Jesus prayer."

She paused, seemed to consider saying more, and then added, "It's really '*Jesus Christ, son of the living God, have mercy on me, a sinner,*' but you can just say 'Have mercy.'"

Not only wasn't I ready to acknowledge any son of the living God, but I had no interest in introducing the word *sinner*, or the concept behind it, into my already-all-too-eager-to-cast-blame mind. "I don't really believe in sin," I told her. Why not go the whole nine yards? This woman was solid. I liked her. More important, I trusted her. "I don't think I have any," I continued. "I mean, that's probably a sin, thinking I don't . . ."

She raised an eyebrow.

"I have trouble with the word," I clarified. "It doesn't feel like it pertains to me. I'm not saying I'm perfect or error-free, I just can't think of any sin. It's so laden, so Catholic-sounding."

"Culturally, it's a complicated word," Pamela said. "It has a lot of baggage. But it's really very simple: Sin means separation from God. We're all sinners. It doesn't mean we're murderers or liars or cheats. Separation from God manifests itself in many ways. Society's standards and God's are very different." She clasped her hands on her lap, gave a gentle nod, and then leaned forward, as though to emphasize a key point. "Start with prayer," she said. "No matter what words you use, God's love is there."

I walked home wondering how she could know that. I walked home wondering where, exactly, was *there*.

THE NEXT MORNING, I woke at four A.M. as usual. The squirrels thumped overhead. Increasing gray pressed against the windows as I burrowed under the musty covers to will away the dawning day. No good.

Pamela had given me the words, but I had to use them.

How?

My stomach seized, and I curled into a fetal position. I saw myself as if from above. What was my problem? What was stopping me? I was alone in my apartment. No one could see me. No parental approval was at stake. The bed wasn't going to liquefy or vanish beneath me. Quiet scared me, pressing emptiness back at me from the windows. Anxiety was awful, but it kept that emptiness at bay, replaced it with its own pressure. The trick, I knew, would be to keep my mind from making too much noise. My head swirled with doubts, but my heart craved solace. *Here goes.*

Prayer. I turned the word around in my mouth, as if tasting the idea. My stomach knotted again, and I tasted the sour trickle that signaled dry heaves. I dashed down the hall.

Back in bed, I tried again. *Prayer.* It was a lovely-sounding word, if I could think of it as just a word. Maybe it wasn't so different from what my parents had told me. *I find God in nature. Faith is a personal thing.* If I was going to find out, I was going to have to jump.

Undeniable daylight shone through the curtains. Time to get up, put on coffee, go into the shower, force down a spoonful or two of Cream of Wheat.

A bird trilled.

"You are there," I whispered.

That was true. The bird was there. The bird and I shared the same moment, in fact, breathed the same air. Light slanted in past the edge of my curtains, whose fabric billowed in a breeze.

"You are *here,*" I whispered, and then, even more quietly, "I am here."

That's true, too, the room bounced back. *Keep going.*

I took a breath. "You"—the birds, the breeze, the air—"are here." I looked down at my legs, drawn up to my chest. My familiar knees, the scar on my calf from eighth grade when I picked a scab for months: "I am here." I left "God" out of it, as I repeated the simple statement. "You are here, I am here."

CHAPTER TWO

*Verily, verily, I say unto thee, We speak that
we do know, and testify that we have seen.*
JOHN 3:11 (KING JAMES BIBLE)

Every morning, as I repeated the prayer and got used to the shape of its words in my mouth, I noticed something. The words, unlike *Hallowed be thy name,* unlike *My soul to take,* were concrete. The literal meaning of *I am here* was incontestable fact, a platform on which I could stand to view the second phrase. *You are here* didn't invite another being as much as acknowledge that it was already there, like calling out "Morning!" to someone in the next room. If I prefaced the statement with *God,* I was submerged in doubts and second thoughts. But if I thought of *You* as the wind and birdsong and squirrels, it eased the tight knot of isolation and took me, however briefly, out of myself.

Rules and structure had kept me safe as a child. When life didn't present enough guidelines, I created my own. For fun, I made up forms just to fill them out. On summer days when my brother and I were children, our mother drove us to Auntie

Claire's house for an afternoon of egg salad and swimming in the pool. To get there, we passed San Quentin. The prison's large yellow building wasn't what fascinated me, or the towers with their huge lights and 360-degree windows, the Cyclone fences with concertina wire, Dad's story of one night seeing a man jump the fence and run. What tugged and beckoned at me were the small, boxy houses with their tidy back lawns abutting the fence through which I saw tricycles and laundry lines with fluttering pillowcases and shirts. Guards and their families lived in those houses, Mom told us, and I wanted to live with them in that promise of order and safety, the grown-up equivalent of playing house.

Wide open space awed and terrified me; as a two-year-old, I spent the drive from San Luis Obispo to Santa Barbara along picture-postcard Highway 1 with my head in my mother's lap to avoid seeing the Pacific. I screamed when my mother ran into the waves at Stinson Beach. I folded my body into my wicker laundry hamper to read picture books to myself and to my dolls and crawled into my baby brother's crib. I liked containment.

The space that prayer now opened around me felt as terrifying as the Pacific once had, but repeating "I am here, You are here" allowed me a way into it. As the day went on, my anxiety didn't vanish. I still had to get up and make my breakfast and force down a few slices of banana and spoonfuls of Cream of Wheat. I still had to drive to San Francisco to teach and drive back to Berkeley to clock hours proofreading classified ads at the *East Bay Express.* But, if only for as long as it took to whisper the words *"You are here,"* I would forget about my tense jaw, my cramping stomach, my fidgeting hands, the *what ifs* of my imagination. As I went about my day, prayer felt a little like a new haircut, stopping me every time I caught a glimpse of myself. But soon I began to stumble into calm.

And then, one morning, it hit like a blow: *This is what happened with Blake.*

I LIVED MY first six years at 15 Bayview Avenue. A single-story three-bedroom house with a carport, it nestled among trees in the front and opened to a yard and the steep slope of a hill in the back. I discovered the world in that house: the infinite wonder of a backyard; the fearsome thrill of Dr. Bennet arriving in the middle of the night to give me a shot that my mother soothingly repeated would make my earache go away; the comfort of Holly, our poodle, whose nails tangled in my hair as I scrunched closer to her warm belly; my mother's taut stomach when she pressed my ear to it and told me to listen for my little brother or sister. I was three when she miscarried, and I don't remember being taken in the middle of the night to the Mills house up the street or what explanation I was given when my mother, no longer pregnant, came to get me. But I do remember, as far back as I can recall, how—despite my make-believe friends who lived in the rhododendron bushes (Morra and Murra, their names distinguished by the tiniest nuance of pronunciation, enough to get me to stamp my feet in indignation when my parents got it wrong); despite Johnny and Paul and Annie Regin, next door; despite Jenny Stiles, with whom I walked hand in hand to kindergarten, and Carolyn Barnes, whose mother wore paper dresses—I wanted a sibling.

When my parents told me there would be a new baby, I felt satisfied and very excited. *At last,* I thought. Two children, two adults—it had such symmetry, and my little sibling-to-be, I knew, would play on my team. My mother's tummy wasn't getting any bigger and I didn't know the word *adoption,* although I'm sure my mother explained it to me in some age-appropriate way. I didn't care where the baby came from. All I knew was that I was getting what I wanted.

There was a boy in my kindergarten class named Blake, and one night as my parents did the dishes, Dad asked, "How about Clay if it's a boy?"

"Clay is a nice name," Mom said. "Or Brad."

I piped up, "What about Blake?"

They stopped what they were doing and looked at me, and then at each other. Slow grins spread across their faces. "Blake," they said together. "Blake Crittenden. That's it!"

Not long before, my mother had asked me what else I thought the new baby would need—she'd already listed a changing table, a nightlight, receiving blankets, a tub for bathing—and I announced, "Love." From the beginning I had no doubt my brother was all mine and I could lavish my care on him. I was a child, too, my logic went, so I knew best what was needed.

When we drove to the hospital the day after he was born, I had to sit in the waiting room while my parents went through a door marked NO ONE UNDER 16 ALLOWED. Sixteen seemed unfathomably far away as I thumbed through *Newsweek* and *Time,* looking for pictures or puzzles—there were no *Highlights* or *Ranger Rick*s in this waiting room. And then the waiting was over and my parents came through the door holding a little bundle and pulled back the blankets to show me his scrunched red face.

My parents taught me how to hold him and how to angle the bottle and how to avoid the soft spot on his head, which I pressed when they weren't looking. I helped bathe his body with PhisoHex. I cut two Ts from corduroy scrap and sewed them together with a fat needle and yarn from my crochet-for-kids kit, to make him a shirt. I crawled into his crib and read to him and played with his fingers and toes and treated him like a live doll.

He played on my team, all right, but he was different, too, and this fascinated me. When his penis struck me as too floppy, I taped it down with a big square Band-Aid. I didn't know that the penis had any other function than that of shooting admirably high-arced streams of pee, but I was concerned that the wobbly sac of skin, the pudgy flaccid finger—so different from my private parts, all tucks and folds—needed protection. He wailed as our mother peeled the Band-Aid off his baggy little scrotum, slowly rather than the fast yank she used on my skinned knees, telling me it would hurt less that way. I felt more fascinated than chastised as she told me, "Don't do that again. The penis is the most sensitive part of the male body."

I loved watching him sleep and lifting the paper-thin lids to see his brown eyes roll. From where I sat, in his crib, a picture book propped against my knees, I could see into the backyard with its lawn and patio table and carefully tended beds. Morra and Murra lived in the rhododendrons still, with their dog Peek-Peek, but I didn't need them anymore. My world felt complete.

A WEEK BEFORE my seventh birthday, when my brother was nine months old and just starting to climb out of his crib (another difference: he couldn't stay still; I loved to), we moved up the hill to a bigger house. I left Jenny and Carolyn behind for a neighborhood where there were lots of old people. Now I walked myself to school, although I found out many years later that my father had followed me the first week to make sure I wouldn't get lost. Our new home had two of the three things I most wanted at age seven from a house: stairs and wall-to-wall carpeting (if not the third, a swimming pool). It had a dusty, cobwebby basement, closets big enough to hide in, and large bedrooms for me and Blake where we built houses out of cardboard blocks and Lincoln Logs and where, one day when he was two, he peed on me. (Later we would say he was getting back at me for taping him down.) And it had a hilly backyard overgrown with bay trees and ivy and poison oak, which we called the Jungle.

One lazy afternoon in my tenth year, I lay on my two-tone pink shag rug, reading. Blake was in the Jungle with Bob, his best friend. Mom and Dad were in their bedroom, napping as they always did on weekend afternoons. David Cassidy sang from my turntable, over and over, "I think I love you."

I heard Bob's frantic voice approach from outside, and then the front door slam and footsteps run up the stairs. "Lindsey!" Bob appeared, panting, in my doorway. "Blake fell! He said to get you. He said not to get your parents! He said to get you!"

I put down my book and followed Bob into the Jungle, where Blake lay on his back beneath a big oak. We were learning first aid in Mrs. Miller's fifth-grade class, so I ordered Bob to lift Blake's ankles and not touch his head. I ascertained that my brother was breathing and awake, but I worried about a broken back. "Don't get up!" I ordered. "Bob, you stay with him!"

The urgency of the situation swelled me with importance, and I ignored my brother's plea not to waken our parents. My dad followed me down to the tree, where he proceeded to lift Blake's arms while he told me to carry his feet.

"No, Daddy!" I insisted. "They say in first aid you should never move someone . . . and never let someone's back sway."

"Shush!" he told me. "Just be quiet and lift him. His back's not broken."

We carried him up the path, my resentment swelling, and into the house. Bob and his slobbery dog, Rodney, tagged after us. Dad lay Blake on the bright orange couch in the den, where I sat with him and brought him cookies and milk. Bob and Rodney went home. My mother appeared, hovering. "Do you think we should go, Jim?" she asked my father.

Of course you shouldn't go, I responded silently, but my father said, "I don't see why not. He'll be fine."

So my parents went. Some party, some neighborhood gathering, my aunt and uncle's house for Sunday-night cocktails—I don't recall where, but I recall my indignation that they did so.

I was a klutz, afraid of the ball, a scaredy-cat. I ran like a girl. (I *was* a girl, I'd retorted silently to the fifth-grade tough who'd so accused me.) To avoid Steal the Bacon or Nation Ball (a game the object of which was to hit an opponent with a large red medicine ball), I hid from PE in the library with a Laura Ingalls Wilder book. "You have no reason to be tired," Mom used to say when I hunkered down in the backseat and picked a drying scab on my knee. But "tired" was the only word I could think of for the dread of facing PE again. "Off you go," she'd tell me, a hand between my shoulder blades as I rubbed the sole of my right Keds into the front step as if to anchor myself there. Mom didn't believe in babying, or mollycoddling, or any kind of fuss. She was affectionate, loving, and generous with the cinnamon toast and bouillon when you were legitimately ill or hurt; but if you were besieged with day-to-day anxiety or social insecurity? She had gotten through tuberculosis at age eighteen by staying strong, by not feeling sorry for herself, and she wanted to shape her children into people who wouldn't be cowed by the world.

Blake didn't shy from ball games in PE. He led the pack in dares and feats, cutting up the fields with bicycle treads and the pavement with sneakers he went through as fast as if they were potato chips. He never faked a sore throat to stay in bed, as I did, although he always came into my room and played cards with me when he got home on days I was sick. He'd fallen from a tree that day, yes—and he was fine. But I figured he must want what I wanted. He was a child, too. So I took seriously my job ministering to him that afternoon, as we lay on the green rug and curled in a crocheted afghan from my bed, eating Chips Ahoy!s and watching old Westerns on channel 2. And my conviction that I knew best what he needed was sealed.

I HAD GIVEN Blake his first name, but the naming in our household didn't begin and end there. My father called me Pieface (or just Pie) until I went to college; my brother was Blake Black in the days he wore a play holster around his narrow hips and Tigger after he announced, one fancy New Year's Eve when our parents splurged on an elegant French restaurant for the four of us, "Tiggers don't like pâté"; later, my mother would call my nephew Snizzlefritz or Ignatz. Even the cat was Burmaspring Elizabeth; the dog who succeeded Holly, Vanilla Woofer Tweeter.

Blake and I had nicknames for each other: Elbert Gilbert Wally (even this had a nickname of its own, Elbie Gilbie); Bothistle; Limpickle. We made them up in the back of the car, on long road trips, and they stuck, both in their full form and their abbreviations. The words were silly, playful; no one other than we seemed to find them amusing. But we didn't care. They weren't for anyone else. Their unique intonation—"Elbie" brought with it a southern twang; "Bothistle" (with the accent on the second syllable) mandated a forced stuffiness—was meant only for us, like a secret handshake in a crowded room, a signal that no matter what the situation (a boring visit with an elderly relative; stiff silence between our parents in the front seat; even a push-and-shove match between ourselves), we had each other. When we were most relaxed, sharing a package of Chips Ahoy!s as we watched *Gilligan's Island* or, later, played Scrabble, I called him Bo and he called me Pick.

Over the years, I became what my high school termed an Organic and he went punk. I went off to college and moved to New York City for a career in publishing, and he dropped out of high school to take the GED and enroll in a series of junior colleges. I got promoted and edited magazines; he accumulated speeding tickets that turned into six weeks' probation for possession of whatever was found in the glove compartment. I settled into a one-bedroom apartment in Greenwich Village with monthly maintenance fees while he hopped from girlfriend to girlfriend and apartment to apartment, losing our father's security deposits. I got used to his not returning my phone calls. He held jobs as a bicycle messenger and backpack exporter and kept an alias (Derringer) on his mailbox. Over those years, our nicknames would fade in usage. But they would never go away.

IN DAVIS, CALIFORNIA, where I began attending grad school in 1993, the crows that roost in trees are most noticeable at dawn and dusk. At dawn, their raucous caw wakes you before it is even light. And at dusk, they fill the trees like black globs of ink until they break apart to swoop and dip. During my first week in Davis, I appreciated the crows for the gothic edge they lend to an otherwise bland university town, but in the months to follow I would grow to hate their raw, insistent caws.

It wasn't the crows that woke me that first Saturday in my new apartment but the phone, ringing just before eight o'clock. "I'm sorry to wake you," my mother said. "But I have some bad news."

It can't be Blake, I thought. *She sounds so calm.*

And then she said it was Blake, that there'd been an accident and he was in the hospital, and I thought, *I'd better sit down.* And then she said it: "He's been shot."

There were details: He was being operated on to relieve the pressure on his brain. The bullet was lodged behind his eye. My parents, who'd spent the night in Sonoma, were headed back to the city and S.F. General.

When I hung up the phone, I trembled in a strange sort of way, as if I were shivering from cold my body didn't yet quite feel. Only later would I realize I didn't feel temperature all day— I didn't need a sweater, despite the damp chill of January rain, and yet I wasn't able to stop shaking, a ceaseless tremor that felt all under the skin because when I looked at my hands they did not move. My friend Janet was visiting with her baby from Southern California, and as I stood in the doorway of the bedroom—I'd given her and the baby my bed and slept in the living room—I said, "I'm really disappointed. I was looking forward to showing you around Davis, maybe going into Woodland for Mexican food."

"Lindsey," she said, kicking off the sheets and hitching the baby higher on her shoulder as she stood, "you need to be in San Francisco."

"They're operating. They'll know more in an hour or so." I could not make sense of the information I'd been given or how to put it in sync with the world around me. I'd last seen my brother on January 2, the previous Sunday, when he had helped me move into a new apartment. After years in and out of drug treatment, he'd found a new program out on Taraval Street, near Ocean Beach, where he used to surf before he sold his board for drug money. He'd been living there for the four months that had coincided with my first term of grad school, and we'd spoken daily. He'd talked with passion and a new, heartening focus about his part-time job trimming trees. "Hey, hanging from a tree with a live chainsaw around my belt is the safest thing I can do," he told me, and compared to the alternative, he was right.

He had a bumper sticker—I ♥ TREES—on his car, a beat-up old Cadillac that made our mother cringe. I'd watched that bumper sticker disappear as his car pulled away from the Ryder Van lot the previous Sunday, and I'd known something was wrong. I could still feel his arms around me. I didn't know then it would be the last time I'd feel them; I only knew he'd hugged me awfully hard as he said, "See ya, sista." *Well,* I told myself as I watched his long, black car turn a corner five blocks away, *I'll see him soon.* When I saw the death certificate a year later, at the Office of Records at City Hall, the words that doubled me over in pain were not *Homicide* or *Gunshot wound to head.* Those said nothing about my brother. The word that made me ache was typed into the space for Occupation. Like the word *brother,* it spoke of hope and sweetness and infinite promise. *Arborist,* it said. For those four months, it had seemed feasible.

And then, as those four months drew to a close, I saw a familiar glassiness return to my brother's brown eyes. I found him dozing in front of the fireplace in the middle of the day and noticed how tense his shoulders looked at Christmas dinner and heard the false cheer in his voice as he wished me a happy New Year when he called to finalize our moving-day plans. My parents and I didn't know then that he'd been kicked out of the Twelve-Step program and was living in his car, but we knew he was using again.

"Lindsey," Janet repeated. "We need to go to San Francisco. Get dressed. I'll drive."

In the shower, I felt and did not feel the water. I wanted to pull it toward me, as if I could hold it to me, and yet it ran through my fingers and down my body. My feet flushed red from the heat of the water and steam, but I didn't feel a thing. "Now rinse," I told myself after lathering with soap, as though I might otherwise forget. I thought, *I will never forget this day.* I thought, *The next shower I take will be in a different world.*

It rained the entire 75 miles from Davis to San Francisco. Janet drove my car exactly 55 mph as her baby screamed in the backseat and I watched the storm clouds move west, following us or leading us, I couldn't be sure. I thought of the phone call I'd made the Wednesday before, telling him that I knew he was in trouble and scared and that I loved him and knew he could be clean again. "I'm here," I told his voice mail. "I'm always here."

I HADN'T ALWAYS been. For years, during the repeated cycle of his using and stealing and lying, Blake and I had rarely spoken. I'd tried, but my efforts had seemed as clumsy and ineffectual as the copy of *Catcher in the Rye* I'd left on his pillow when he was in high school and I visited one weekend from college, just to have him refer to it later as "that lame book about that lame preppy."

In 1986, my brother visited me in New York, where he admitted over burgers and fries at the Old Town Saloon on West Eighteenth Street that he'd tried crack, telling me, "Calm down, hon, I can handle it," and then insisting it was all a CIA plot to keep down inner-city blacks anyway. He spent a month in Marin County Jail, a month during which I sent him a postcard every day (the postcards were all of fish, for reasons I can't recall; I just recall going every morning to a card shop near my office to buy a new one). He used Dad's ATM card (the PIN was laughably obvious, the password they used for everything, the year of their marriage) and broke into our parents' house, tripping the wires after they changed *that* password to steal the wallet from beneath our sleeping father's head. In 1989, after our father's job as general counsel was relocated to corporate headquarters in Atlanta, Blake followed Mom and Dad there with his girlfriend of two months, who was pregnant. Blake and Sheryl were married on our parents' back lawn, and a week later, my parents told Blake that if he didn't get help for his addiction they'd pull the financial plug. Blake agreed, but when told that a place was waiting for him at Brawner, a nearby rehab facility, and that tomorrow wasn't good enough, he threw a chair at my father. The orderlies were waiting outside, and my brother was taken to Brawner in a straightjacket. Two weeks later, he ran away. Sheryl picked him up in Mom's car at a pre-arranged spot on the county road, where the Brawner staff had no jurisdiction, and the two of them headed downtown for drugs. When my mother expressed concern over Sheryl's being pregnant, Blake told Mom, "It doesn't matter, because the baby is so little." My brother, in other words, had become a full-blown addict.

He acknowledged my postcards, but never returned my phone calls. The few times I reached him, he was running out the door and said he would call me back. He didn't. When I tried talking to him in person about what he was doing, he answered me in platitudes or grunts or patronizing references to the jokes that had flowed between us as children yet now no longer made me even smile.

My brother had an innate, precise sense of humor. He dubbed Mom and Dad's lectures "stereophonic maul." He'd named his cat, a stray he took in during his brief college stint in San Diego who moved with him everywhere after that, Burden. Because of the motorcycle cops in their stormtrooper boots hiding behind the bushes to clock housewives going 41 in a 40 mph zone, Tiburon Boulevard, the main drag between our childhood house and the freeway, became the "boulevard of fear." One day, when I visited San Francisco from New York, he and I drove up to Twin Peaks to gaze over the city and the Bay through a thick brown layer of Indian summer smog. We were tiptoeing around each other—not talking about the bong on his coffee table or the fact that he had three VCRs—and he broke the tension by saying, "Well, hon, looks like someone in Alameda's got a really bad cough."

But as his addiction worsened and the lies increased, his jokes made me purse my lips and look sour at what I felt was pretense and degradation of all that had been good inside him. He had always carried an easy charm, an ability to make even the grown-ups laugh (one of whom, I later found out, said, "This kid's either going to be president or going to end up in jail"), and no one had been more susceptible than our mother. She often quoted his shrink at Brawner, who admitted his struggle not to be won over by Blake's humor. Since childhood, Blake had charmed his way out of her disapproval. As the older sister (the responsible one, as I was constantly reminded), I had always resented what he got away with and was quick to recognize his behavior as manipulation—especially as his addiction worsened—and my mother's response as denial and collusion. One Easter, as he and Mom engaged in one-upping each other on listing what she termed his escapades—climbing out of his crib at nine months; pouring Dad's Scotch down the drain at two or three; scaling the north tower of the Golden Gate Bridge when he was sixteen; throwing off the radar guns of those Tiburon cops with tin foil stuffed in the wheels of his used Vespa—I stood up mid-anecdote and cleared my place.

He found me in the kitchen, loading the dishwasher. "You haven't been excused, hon," he said, and as I ignored him, "Jeez, what's your problem? You've lost your sense of humor. You've gotten so uptight."

I turned, met his gaze. "My sense of humor's just fine when something is funny." I shut the dishwasher and walked away.

I walked around, during those years, with a constant pit in my stomach. When friends asked about Blake, I changed the subject. When men pursued me, I met once or twice for lunch or a movie, always insisting on going Dutch, and then, when they called again, lied that I was busy or getting back with an old boyfriend. I cried once in three years, and that was while watching Samuel Jackson suck on a crack pipe during a preview of *Jungle Fever*.

I felt bludgeoned, numbed, shell-shocked by my brother's addiction, by his showing up at our parents' with a pregnant girl-friend, by their decision to have the baby despite the obvious obstacles, by my parents' insistence on their marrying and Dad's repeated financial bailing out, by Mom's Saturday phone calls inevitably beginning with "the latest on your brother."

And then, one spring day, after my brother had broken into our parents' house three times in two weeks, I called him. I had a phone in my office on East Fiftieth Street, but I'd gone to the pay phone in the lobby to make the call because I didn't want any of my colleagues to overhear. Blake and Sheryl were living at her father's apartment, a twenty-minute drive from our parents' house in San Francisco, from which Blake had stolen limited-edition books, jewelry, and cash.

The phone rang, and Sheryl answered.

"It's Lindsey," I told her. "I need to talk to my brother."

"You don't have to be rude," she said.

"I'll be anything I want to be. Get Blake."

The phone dropped, there was rustling, and then Blake's groggy voice said, "Yeah."

My heart was thumping, my mouth dry, but years of silence burst forth. Something had snapped in me, and all the fury I'd been too stunned to admit suddenly held an undeniable adrenaline. "What the fuck," I shouted, "do you think you're doing?"

"What the hell." From his tone, I could imagine his mouth curled in disgust, his hardened eyes, the face of an addict and felon whose displeasure I'd avoided for years because it scared me. Now it fed my fury.

"You know exactly what I'm talking about, you little fuck. Why do you break into Mom and Dad's house? Why do you hurt the only people who love you? Why don't you just break into the corner store? Why don't you take a gun to your head and save everyone a lot of trouble?"

"Calm down, hon." His voice oozed into its other, equally infuriating tone.

"Don't you dare patronize me."

There was silence then, and I could hear Sheryl's voice in the background, whether berating me or him I couldn't tell.

His voice went flat. "I got to go." He hung up.

I emerged, shaking, from the phone booth, and the man behind the candy counter stared at me as though I were a live cobra. I left the building and walked around the block, amazed but not particularly relieved. That was a Friday.

My mother left me a weepy message Sunday morning, to the effect that thanks to me Blake had turned himself in. I got the real story that night, when he called me collect from jail. He'd been pulled over for a broken brake light and been found to have several outstanding warrants. He was sobbing. "Thank you for your call the other day," he said. "You told me what I needed to hear."

I slid down the wall of my kitchen to sit on the floor with the phone pressed against my ear. We stayed on the phone for hours as he told me how miserable he was, how awful his life had become, how horrible he felt, how scared he was that he'd never get better, how afraid he was that he'd never be able to be a father to his son. I listened, tears rolling down my cheeks. "You know," he told me at one point, with a kind of amazed innocence, "I never thought of the corner store."

That was in early 1992, and seven months later, at Thanksgiving, I visited him at Redwood House, a resident drug rehab facility in Redwood City. That day, he made me laugh again. That day, we dipped into the pool of familiar nicknames and jokes as if into clean, fresh water. As we walked the hills of the property, among the manzanita and madrone, he spoke about his addiction and about our childhoods. We played badminton and sat on a picnic table, talking. Blake admitted to having what he called a humor mask and to his difficulty accepting the first step. When I heard him say, "I finally get it. I finally admit I am powerless over drugs," I didn't hear the jargon. I heard my brother, speaking the truth. The sky above us was clear and blue, the light low with late-autumn sun. I did not think of the word *resurrection,* but now, as I write this, I can't not.

Yet, that day, I also felt skepticism. *Trust, but verify.* My brother was good at telling you what you wanted to hear, and part of me would always hold back. When he suggested we take his son, Dylan, then two and a half, camping in Yosemite the following summer, I said, "Sounds good, but let's just focus on today. Summer's a long way off." I was always mindful of the potential of relapse; Redwood House, after all, was his third (and a year later, would become his fourth) rehab program. But that Thanksgiving Day in 1992, we were both high on the promise of recovery.

One Saturday, a month before he was shot, he and I were at our parents' place in Sonoma—I was in the small shed we called an office writing a paper for a grad school seminar and he was thirty feet up in a bay tree with a chain saw. On my way into the house for another cup of coffee, I walked below him.

"Heads, Pick!"

I looked up. A tree limb swayed from the rope he'd rigged. His chest bare on the warm December day, a chain saw dangling from his belt, he looked the picture of a handsome, muscled twenty-five-year-old, which he was. Clean and sober for ninety days and counting, he grinned at me with pure, unmistakable pleasure and fondness. He hadn't called me Pick in years.

"Bo-thiss-ull!" I called up, the phrasing as familiar to me as if I'd never stopped saying it.

"Lim-pick-le," he responded, note for note.

There was a time when we'd used those names as casually as if we were asking for the salt, but now we knew their significance. Now, after almost eight years of estrangement during which those nicknames sat unspoken between us like a taunt, a reprimand, a place so painful neither of us went there—now, these names carried a deeper joy because they held redemption, too. As much as the hours-long phone calls, the tears and hugs and letters back and forth, in which I confessed how much his addiction scared and paralyzed me and he wrote *I thank God every day that you are in my life,* those silly names said it all. We could never make up for what we'd lost in those eight years, and for what his death would take away forever. But in those last four months of his life, we had each other back.

I SAT IN my car as Janet drove and I stared at the dark clouds and I said, "Thank God I called him last Wednesday. Thank God I'm not angry at him anymore." I didn't think God had anything to do with it; I used the expression the way I used "Jesus!" when someone cut me off in traffic. They were just words, words of intense if not literally intended meaning. I did not pray for my brother the way I'd once prayed for my cat, not because I loved him less but because I could not think to pray. I couldn't think beyond the words "pressure on the brain." I had no idea what they might mean. I couldn't ask for my brother not to die because I couldn't imagine his dying.

Janet and I pulled up just as my parents were backing out of the garage. The three of us drove to S.F. General. We walked up the steps separately, not touching: my father in a wool jacket and slacks, my mother in a nylon raincoat and sensible shoes, I in sweats with a fraying cord. I saw the three of us then, and I see us now, as if I were floating somewhere in the clouds, which gave off a light drizzle.

We made our way to Ward B, where we'd been told to ring the bell outside the closed double doors. A nurse answered and when my mother said who we were, frowned and asked us to wait. The doors closed again and we each turned to the wall, three private pivots of despair. I hadn't cried until then. The doctor opened the door and gave a terse nod.

"My God!" my mother said. "Tell us: Is he still alive?"

"Yes." The doctor led us to a small conference room. We sat down. He spoke in third person objective, no personal pronouns. The bullet had entered through the back of the skull, just behind the right ear, and lodged in the brain behind the eye socket. There was severe swelling and damage. The pupils did not respond to light. Even with survival, there would be lack of cognition, perception, and motor ability. The body had begun to atrophy.

"Brain dead," I said.

"We prefer not to use that term."

"Oh, my God," my mother said.

My father reached for the square box of Kleenex, took off his glasses, stared at the table.

"Is there any chance?" I asked. "Even a small one?"

"The pupils do not respond to light."

"But—could that change? I mean, what if . . ."

My mother placed her hand on mine. My father pressed a wad of tissue to his face.

My brother, who once said he could see to the Grand Tetons from Tiburon Boulevard, who scored so high on an IQ test that the school wouldn't release the number but enrolled him in MGM, Mentally Gifted Minors—or, as he called it, Mentally Gifted Monsters—was brain dead. His body was useless. The hospital wouldn't take organs from a drug addict.

"I'll leave you alone," the doctor said. "I know you need to discuss it."

The door closed. There was nothing to discuss. We all knew. And when the doctor returned, my father told him, "My son would not have wished to be kept alive artificially. He would not have wanted to live like . . . like that."

The doctor looked each one of us in the eye, and we each looked back.

"You're absolutely sure?" I asked. "There's no chance?"

"He could live for a while. But he would never be the person you knew."

Knew. I looked away.

"My God," my mother said. "My God, what will we tell Dylan. My God, what will we do."

HIS HEAD WAS swaddled in a turban of white gauze and a venti-lator tube was stuck in his mouth, but these are not the things I see when I remember. The ventilator whooshed in an eerie mimic of human breath, a muffled mechanical Darth Vader sound, but what I remember is the silence. The skin of Blake's face was tinged orange from disinfectant; stubble marked his cheeks and chin. His forehead was smooth and broad and bare in a way we had not seen since he'd shaved it to go skinhead in eighth grade, and my parents and I marveled at the handsome brow that had been hidden under his hair. I took in the familiar apostrophe of his sculpted bicep; the broad flat plane of his forearms where they met his wrists; the freckles on his bare shoulders; the curved scar along his right nostril; the long eyelashes he'd cut off at age four with Mom's manicure scissors because women kept telling him how pretty they were; the straight scar under his chin where he took six stitches after banging against the edge of the Morrisons' pool; the flared, almost African, nose; the blackheads inside his ear that I'd once picked at and he at mine, like monkeys. It was my brother lying there, every recognizable feature visible except his thick hair, which had been shaved beneath the white gauze, and his brown eyes, which were closed.

I asked the nurse to lower the bed rail. She came around to where I stood, right against it, and lowered it for me. I'd seen her hold Blake's hand and stroke his arm as she answered our questions, confirmed the doctor's prognosis. I liked her. I asked her to please leave. His third finger was taped to a stint that had a little glowing red light at the end, connected to the heart monitor, she'd said, and when I touched his hand it felt cold and totally without response, so I sat on the bed and bent my forehead to his chest. The nurse had pulled the peach-colored cotton blanket straight across his shoulders. No one sleeps that tidily, that precisely, especially not someone who, the nurse had told us, had kicked and screamed and lashed out as he was rolled in on a gurney. Yet, there was warmth against the waffle weave of the blanket, a warmth that a thermal blanket alone cannot generate. I closed my eyes. I breathed in the warmth. Beneath my forehead, pressed so hard that the weave left hatches there, I felt the ventilator-exaggerated rise and fall of his chest. I said what came naturally. I said, "Goodbye, Bo," and I heard my mother sob.

And then I felt it.

The strongest love I've ever known. A moment of pure, transcendent grace. My brother was not conscious—he would never be conscious again—and yet he felt it, too. I cannot explain that, but I know it. I can write now that the intimacy I felt enveloped in could not have occurred if I'd been alone. I can write now that the warmth I felt depended on two. But what I thought then? Nothing. All I knew was that everything from the moment I had first learned how to hold his body to this pressure of blanket against my forehead passed between us and was shared, acknowledged, forgiven. In that small warm pocket of space, I did not hear my parents' sobs or the *whoosh* of the ventilator. I did not see the orange tint of my brother's skin or his brow beneath the turban of gauze. Everything outside of him and me fell away. Time expanded and stood still. I had never felt such sweetness before, such encompassing light.

BLAKE DIED AT 3:08 P.M. on January 8, 1994, and in the almost three years between that day and the day I visited Pamela, I'd had ample time to reflect on what his loss meant. It meant I was an only child again. It meant, one day when I turned fifty-nine, I would have had as many years without him as with. It meant, as exploitative as it felt to think it, I now had plenty of material to write about. He would never read my work or be an usher at my wedding. His son, who was three at the time of Blake's death, would grow up without a daddy—and I, Dylan's aunt, would play an even larger role in his life, a role I couldn't then imagine. My brother had lost the war on drugs, and I would never be able to smile even the tightest of smiles at any joke involving the word *crack*.

It meant these and all sorts of other thoughts. Some were petty, like the relief I acknowledged at not having to worry about being financially responsible for him in our old age if he was still using. Others felt almost mundane in their stark obviousness, like the moment, on the Davis bike path one hot day, I realized I could no longer recall the exact brown of his eyes.

That moment at his bedside had fed me with something precious. I'd never doubted it. I might have, if I looked at it literally. My brother hadn't responded to my touch or to the beam of the doctor's penlight in his eyes. But my brother had brown eyes while my parents and I had blue, and he was no less my brother. He was adopted, but that mattered less than the fact that, at six, I'd pricked our thumbs with a pin and pressed them together. He couldn't see the Grand Tetons any more than Jack, his alter ego who sometimes showed up at the dinner table in lieu of Blake, had flown a helicopter across the Bay to dine with us. ("Jack," my mother would ask, "would you like Blake's milk or shall I pour you your own?")

I've always been literal-minded, analytic to the point of tedium. At nineteen, living in France, I'd visited the Catholic shrine of Lourdes. As my companions and I trekked into town from the train station, we'd rolled our eyes and snickered at the row of souvenir shops selling holographic postcards of the Virgin Mary and empty plastic bottles bearing the legend *"Je Suis la Conception Immaculée,"* the restaurants advertising Pilgrims' Specials in four different languages. And then, the next day, we approached the grotto itself.

Mary, the story goes, appeared in a niche of rock to a peasant girl called Bernadette in 1858, a repeated visit that resulted in Bernadette's canonization and express trains from Rome to this remote location in the Pyrenees. That day in 1981, we fell in with the crowds of pilgrims in wheelchairs and on crutches, many of them clutching empty bottles and crying out in suffering and ecstasy. Dangling over the grotto like Christmas lights, a string of crutches gave testimony to the cripples who had walked away. Surely this place was rife with what my mother would call the hypocrisy of organized religion, with what my father had implicitly criticized in his statement that faith is a private thing. And yet, I couldn't write the whole thing off. I was fascinated.

A boy in front of me asked his mother, "But how do we know it's real, *Maman?*"

Unlike most of the pilgrims, who were dowdily attired, *Maman* was an attractive woman. I stepped closer to catch her response. She gave a slight shrug and spoke as simply as if she were telling her son to wipe his mouth: *"La foi,"* she said. Faith.

The boy looked satisfied, but I felt more bemused than ever. My companions and I stayed another day in Lourdes, hiking in the hills and picnicking along a verdant stream. *This,* I'd thought, breathing in the fresh mountain air and watching the rain-swollen water, *is what I believe in.* Faith beyond the tactile and concrete seemed too mysterious, too superstitious, too absent of thinking. Fifteen years later, it still did.

And yet as I sat in my Berkeley bedroom and watched my curtains suck in and out the open window, I knew proof was beside the point. I'd never been able to prove what I felt at my brother's hospital bed, either—and I'd never needed to. Death reduces love to its essential, and there—in essence—is where we find God.

CHAPTER THREE

Open my lips, O LORD, and my mouth
shall proclaim your praise.

PSALM 51:16

Virginia in July is hot and, in the foothills of the Blue Ridge, sultry. But in the early morning, as I walked the dirt road gutted from nightly thunderstorms, the air held freshness. In another hour, the chicory would have closed up its petals against the heat, but for now its blue blossoms were open and glinting with dew. In the field to my left, cows raised their heads to watch me as they chewed, steadily moving toward the fence to keep between me and the calf born two days earlier.

Life back in Berkeley was feeling more settled, as I got used to planning it out in six-month chunks of freelance gigs and teaching contracts. I made professional headway writing for a local paper, getting some stories published, and winning an award. I found a new pool, an outdoor one, with black marble facing its deep-end wall. I went there daily, loving the structure of its black lines, the back-and-forth hypnosis of laps, the pillars of sunlight refracting through water or pebbles of rain hitting the surface, the feeling of my body moving the way it was made to.

Long after Nation Ball and Steal the Bacon went the way of striped Danskin coordinates and hand-printed report cards, I'd stayed a klutz. When I was in college, no one I knew "worked out," but I'd graduated and moved to New York City during the era of Jane Fonda in leg warmers. I'd gone to aerobics studios blasting "Moon Rocks" and "Billie Jean." I'd tripped over my own two feet and gotten booming headaches. And then, one day on my way to the locker room at the Brooklyn Y, I'd passed the pool. So inviting! And swimming was something I knew I could do.

I'd grown up around pools: my auntie Claire's, where I bounced on my mother's ankle as she sat on the steps of the shallow end; the Morrisons', down the street, always heated to a bathtublike ninety degrees; the club, where I'd learned to swim by diving down to the bottom of the shallow end for a rock painted with my name. I'd loved Marco Polo and underwater tea parties and floating and turning handstands in the shallow end. I stayed in water until my fingers puckered like raisins. But it wasn't until the Brooklyn Y that I became a swimmer.

The first day, I made it only five lengths before I had to stop, chest heaving and breath ragged. When, after a month, I made it twenty-five laps, exhilaration and adrenaline flooded me. So this was what all the fuss was about! I might as well have crossed the English Channel.

In Berkeley, I swam every day. I saw my parents and Dylan frequently—once a week or so—but family, increasingly, felt *there* and work *here.* Writing was all mine, free of the tug of obligation I often felt, as a single person and now only child, toward my parents and nephew. Never was this more the case than when I was on residency, as I was now in Virginia.

Create in me a clean heart, O God, and renew a right spirit within me.

Prayer, too, was helping to ground me in a life of my own in the Bay Area. I was going to All Souls every Sunday, though I continued to hold back from communion. Instead, I lined up in a side pew for healing prayers. I bowed my head to receive the blessing, soaking up the touch of a hand on my hair, the glide of the priest's fingers on my forehead as they marked the sign of the cross with oil. I went to Epiphany services and Lenten discussion groups and helped out at the All Souls soup kitchen.

My parents never said much about my going back to church— "Meet anyone interesting?" Mom would ask, as though I'd been to a cocktail party, and Dad would only offer up "Huh." I was used to keeping my personal life from my parents—from Mom because if I mentioned meeting a man, for example, then I would have to field questions for weeks; from Dad because Dad and I just didn't talk about personal stuff then. Prayer wasn't dating, but it held the same squirm factor of revelation. Nor had I ever told my parents about what I'd felt at Blake's deathbed. They'd been with me in the room, of course, and I didn't want to seem to top their experience with mine. I couldn't explain my new interest in prayer, and the permission and urgency I felt to explore it further, without describing what I'd felt with Blake. So I kept it to myself.

Prayer, for me, had begun in bed—as a child, pleading with God to take care of my cat; as an adult, wrestling with anxiety. As I continued praying, though, I felt the need to get up. Bed was too comfy and pillowed, too reminiscent of other activities. So I sat on the floor, wedging my body into the space between the bed, a table, a chair, and the wall. The hardness beneath me was reassuring, and I tucked into the tight space just as I had once tucked into my laundry basket to look at a picture book. I felt safe and small, protected and private. I repeated the words "You are here, I am here" for only five minutes. But in those five minutes, something opened up inside of me, something I had not believed possible. A kind of spaciousness, even as my knees began to tingle from being drawn up to my chest. By getting physically small, I began to loosen. It didn't make sense, but maybe it didn't have to.

Pamela introduced me to a Centering Prayer group, which met weekly in the darkened All Souls chapel. We'd begin with a gospel reading, a chant, and—this being Berkeley—some yoga. And then we'd sit in meditative silence for twenty minutes. I amazed myself by being able to let my mind go, to stop thinking—if only long enough to realize I'd stopped. One day, I had a vision of a bearded, dark-skinned man. Jesus? I had a hunch it wasn't my seventh-grade science teacher. This stunned me: Was I going to start "witnessing"? Was I going to turn fundamentalist? But the feeling had been so sweet and accepting that I held on to it, although I didn't tell anyone. My prejudices about belief were tenacious.

The anxiety lifted, but it didn't vanish overnight. One day, I came home from running the stadium steps. I've never liked to run, but that day I needed to pound my feet into something. Back at my front door, I still felt jangled and tight. I walked into the living room and flopped onto the floor. The words spilled forth: *"The LORD is my shepherd; I shall not want. He maketh me to lie down in green pastures; he leadeth me beside the still waters."*

I'd heard the King James version of the Twenty-third Psalm my whole life, but I wasn't used to hearing it in my own voice. Now the words came unbidden, the very enunciation of them through my lips summoning release. I lay on my back, tears creeping into my hairline.

Another day I was in the car at a stoplight. The winter sun glared low and penetrating through the windshield; next to my little Honda, a hulking SUV seemed to abrade my bare skin. I'd be home in five minutes, where the walls waited to bounce back at me. My stomach knotted, I tasted metal. I thought I might throw up. At any second, the light would turn green and I'd have to drive through. How? Why?

Maybe, I thought, *I should pray.*

Pamela nodded when I told her this over tea, as if she'd expected as much. "God's speaking to you. Whenever you think of prayer, God's giving you a hint."

Wait a minute. *Maybe I should pray* had been my idea! I recognized my "should" of obligation, my "maybe" of hesitation. God spoke in thunder and burning bushes, not in tremulous *what if*s. I believed in free will, ever since I'd stood in the kitchen, staring at the hem of my mother's twill skirt, as she imparted some lesson about picking up my toys or not picking the scab that bled into my best dress-up socks. Her broad, capable hands held me by the shoulders: Did I understand?

I nodded. I understood perfectly. She was the authority. And I made a vow: *I will never forget what it is to be the child. I will never forget what I know.* It was automatic, and yet I felt the thrill of articulating that I could go to a place where I wouldn't be followed or watched.

Now Pamela was suggesting not only that God could follow me there but that God ran the place.

I didn't buy it.

I'd never had a lover or a friend with whom I could be consistently, completely honest. The freest relationship I'd had was with Blake, and look where that had gotten me. Now Pamela was introducing the concept of God as someone, some*thing,* who knew all of me, whether I acknowledged God or not. And not in the formal, best-behavior stance that I'd always assumed was the basis for devotion. No, this went far deeper and was far scarier.

"Many people pray while driving," Pamela continued. "It makes sense."

Like singing in the shower, I thought—*no one to hear.* Then I caught myself.

I was used to spouting off in the car, just as I had once stood in front of my bedroom mirror with a blanket wrapped around my shoulders in imitation of a designer gown, to give an Oscar acceptance speech in which I'd plead for social justice (in seventh grade, I was equally inspired by the Academy Awards and by having heard King's "I Have a Dream" speech in social studies). On long drives, I whiled away the miles by scripting scenarios occasioned by running into my college boyfriend on the street, going for a drink, and winding up in his hotel room—after which he'd admit to never getting over me. I imagined what Terry Gross and I would talk about when my novel got me on *Fresh Air.* Thinking of myself as seen by an imaginary audience kept me draped in an illusion of significance while keeping me from having to say a thing. I could be myself with this imagined audience only because I knew I was alone.

But God in the passenger seat?

The words of the opening Collect every Sunday refer to a God "to whom all hearts are open, all desires known, and from whom no secrets are hid." So much for keeping things to myself. Pamela was implying the inverse of my fantasies: If I wasn't alone, how could I be myself?

I surprised myself that afternoon over tea. I heard what Pamela said. I listened to my familiar rebuttals, my doubts. And I believed her.

Cast me not away from your presence, and take not your holy spirit from me.

Like any commitment, like any relationship, prayer and I had to get used to each other. Writing had been a good teacher of the unpredictable. I knew how some mornings could flow like honey, hours passing like seconds as I typed away, and how others felt like a unique brand of torture as I stared at the screen, picked my cuticles, got up for a toothpick to clean out the dust between the keys, despaired of ever writing a true sentence again. An uncle had once asked me how I got my ideas for writing: "So do you wait for inspiration to hit, or what?"

If I waited for inspiration, I told him, I'd never write a word.

So with prayer, I knew I couldn't rely on lightning bolts or thunder claps, or even birdsong. I had to make prayer a habit, to go to it the way I went each morning to the desk. Not to summon prayer, but to tap into what was already there.

Thanks to writing, I knew to stick it out. Thanks to writing, I knew to keep praying even if some mornings I got no further than the day's shopping list. I worried, though, that if I prayed first thing in the morning, as I had begun doing, then I would lose my writing discipline. I worried that my creativity would go into prayer, leaving nothing behind for the keyboard. Was I willing to make that trade? I started keeping a notebook by my feet, with a pencil, just in case.

I collected props: candles, large and small, decorative and purely functional; a handout from church with the words to a psalm; a pebble with a perfect waistline of white stripe; sage from the Bighorns, more redolent of dust than of the high plains and tied with string from a Wyoming motel sewing kit; an AA symbol Blake had carved from soapstone. I arranged these items on an old sewing machine cabinet in my bedroom and started praying there, as if at a desk. I wasn't ready to call it a shrine.

When I first lighted the candles, I felt extremely self-conscious. *This is so predictable,* I thought, *so portentous.* I'd started out of pure need, and now I was gathering accoutrements. But then I saw what I was doing: the narrow strip on the edge of the matchbook; the smell of sulfur; the flare of heat, the bright yellow flame. No figment, this. It had a reassuring tactility, a surprisingly familiar primality.

I would have been six or seven when my cousin Greg taught me how to run my finger through a flame. We were gathered around the Thanksgiving table, a place of predictability. Every year, the same menu, the same stinking cigars my uncles smoked, the same rhyming games my aunt played across the table with me. I was a protected child, and running my finger through a flame seemed the height of daring and danger. And Greg was right. Done fast enough, my finger through the flame didn't feel a thing. I was disappointed. Years later, stoned with friends, I would hold my thumbnail to a lighter and feel the same letdown—until I took my thumb away and found the nail yellowed, thickened, and faintly stinking.

I watched the flame flicker. I thought of storms that knocked out the electricity in our house when I was growing up so we had to rummage through a drawer for stubs and tapers of wax, of watching a friend wave her arms over Shabbat candles one Friday evening, of seductions. Candlelight confers significance; we look to a flame to expand possibility, to enrich the moment. Maybe that's what I wanted. I decided to keep the candles lighted.

I kept bumping up against a familiar conviction: If I had the correct components, if I went through the motions properly, everything would fall in place. This belief was full of worry that verged on panic. I'd seen potential ruined before, and I had to do all I could to keep it from happening again. The stakes felt unbearably high.

IN DECEMBER 1990, I'd been living on the East Coast long enough for the hazy sunshine of a California winter to feel utterly foreign, and while I would not have used the word *detachment* to describe the experience of a day Blake and I spent together, that's the overwhelming sensation I remember. Dylan was nine months old, strapped into his car seat, as Blake drove around the city. We stopped at Gordo's on Geary Boulevard for burritos, and at China Beach to eat them.

Afterward, he headed the car to his and Sheryl's apartment on Twin Peaks. We'd been making small talk, polite and distant, all afternoon. Those were the days when we never talked about his addiction; he refused to admit he had a problem, and I played along, telling myself that if he could just get a job and hunker down to his responsibilities as a new father, all would fall into place. I felt so overwhelmed by the enormity of what was at stake—this baby, babbling in the backseat; my brother's survival—that I broke it down into small, manageable components. Such as a job.

"You have any good leads?" I asked as he pulled the car along a curb outside an apartment building stepped into the hill to take advantage of the views. The paint on the curb was faded but unmistakably red. "Can you park here?"

"Just did." He killed the engine and got out, reaching in the backseat for Dylan.

"You might look into taking classes at night," I suggested, scurrying to keep up as he headed into the building. I tried not to rush to any conclusions: a front door open to the street; a dim musty hallway; dark carpet that reminded me of indoor/outdoor carpeting from the 1960s; a hole in the wall outside their apartment, which looked the perfect size and shape to have had the doorknob slammed into it. My brother had a temper, and I thought of how my mother had explained his and Sheryl's move into this apartment from the previous one, out by Ocean Beach, with a detail involving a broken window. "Well, it *is* a better location," she'd clarified. "Closer to a park for the baby."

Blake put the baby, still in his car seat, on the carpeting and slowly pushed in the apartment door, holding up his hand so that my voice, when I spoke, was a whisper. "Smart as you are," I continued, "without a college degree, you have a real liability."

"Babe? You here?" He poked his head in the door, keeping his hand raised. No response, and he lowered his hand as I followed him inside. On the floor was a heap of blankets, and just beyond, a couch. A playpen with blankets and scattered stuffed toys stood in a corner between the TV and a large picture window. The room was tidy and bright, sparely furnished, and I felt a semblance of relief. Blake put Dylan on the floor next to a caged cockatiel, which jerked its gray-tinged-with-orange head at us.

"So pretty," I said. "What's its name?"

"Bird." Blake gave the grin I knew so well, and I felt myself relax a notch. He bent over to place a plastic toy phone in Dylan's hand. And then he swiveled on his heels to crouch near the mound of blankets. "Hey, babe."

He placed his hand on what I now saw was a head, sleek with dark hair.

"I'm back with Dyl." He stroked her hair. "Linds is with me."

She gave a groan and rolled further into the blankets.

"You're okay, babe." His voice was soothing, reassuring, like a parent's to a fevered child. "I'll make you something to eat. Wouldn't that be good?" He kissed her cheek and stood, walked into the kitchen, where he cracked an egg into a pan on the stovetop and pushed a slice of bread into a toaster. I sat on the couch, reaching a finger out to Dylan, who grabbed it as he babbled "Hehwoe" over and over into the plastic phone. I asked Blake about deadlines for City College—they were doubtless approaching, I said, but he could probably enroll if he called right away—and did he have a résumé and I'd be happy to help him pull one together.

"Yeah. Great. Thanks."

He would have said something like that, as I stared out the sliding glass doors at the hazy view of the city and bay and hills beyond. The aroma of browning butter and eggs filled the room. He pulled a fork out of a drawer and carried the food on a plate over to Sheryl, who hadn't moved. He placed it on the carpet next to her face.

I stood to use the restroom. On my way there, I peeked in the bedroom. Maroon curtains over a small window bathed the unmade bed in a dark, vaguely psychedelic light. In the bathroom, Blake's collection of rubber duckies lined the tub. The shower curtain was ripped from a few of the rings holding it up, not unlike—I told myself, as if to balance out the internal checklist I was ticking off, "Signs of Unhealthy Lifestyle"—the shower curtains of friends in college or during my first days in New York. Back in the living area, I noticed a small alcove adjoining the kitchen. On a card table against the short wall, Blake had set up a clock radio, a telephone, a framed photograph of my father taken when he was named general counsel, and an Ansel Adams wall calendar Mom had given Blake for Christmas. As a teenager, Blake had loved photography, setting up a darkroom in a corner of our cobwebby basement. Our parents had given him, for various Christmases, a Nikon, a motor drive, and a telephoto lens, all of which at some point he'd later hocked and then, promising sobriety, got a loan from Dad to buy back. But it wasn't just the Ansel Adams that told me Blake had set up the desk—it was the tidiness, the same tidiness with which my brother had once stacked Christmas packages beneath the tree and later would fit my boxes and furniture into the back of a Ryder truck on the last day I saw him alive, as if a desk arranged just so will let the rest fall into place.

I gave Blake what I hoped was an encouraging smile as we watched Dylan pull himself up onto the couch, where Blake sat. And then I noticed Blake's jiggling knee and, glancing back to the floor, the now cold eggs untouched next to his wife's dark head.

When I was in high school, my mother used to help me study for Spanish tests. She'd sit on the edge of my bed and quiz me on vocabulary, throwing out the words, returning again and again to the ones that slipped me up and sliding in a toughie in the middle of a stretch of easy ones, until I was in good shape for the test. One night as she left my room, I heard my brother call to her and the creak of the floor beneath her step as she went to him.

A minute or two later, she was back in the hallway. "I'd be happy to help you, Blake, but you have to study first."

My brother and I were different—night and day, Mom used to say. I was the good girl, the responsible child; he was the rebel, the charmer. And yet, despite our polar-opposite personalities, we shared from childhood an undeveloped sense of follow-through. To this day, I am in thrall to potential, as though a new job, a New Year's resolution, a haircut is all it takes to achieve the desired outcome. When disappointment strikes, when potential meets reality, I have to fight an awful despair that verges on panic. *Do something,* it says; *do something now.*

When I remember that day on Twin Peaks, it is not the babbling baby or the hole in the wall or the plate of untouched food that haunts me. It is that desk and the longing I saw in it, the longing on my brother's part for legitimacy and purpose and on mine for that brother I had named.

VISITING MY PARENTS one day soon after I had first met Pamela, I noticed a copy of the Book of Common Prayer on a bookshelf, next to the dusty German Bibles from my mother's side of the family. This particular copy—red leather, cracked spine—came from Dad's mother, an ardent and biased Episcopalian. (Once, as we parked in front of the dry cleaners to pick up Daddy's shirts— folded, light starch—I'd heard Grandma tell my mother about some people she knew back in Oregon who, she whispered, "were Presbyterian." It sounded as bad as "divorced," as "drinkers.") I pulled the book from the shelf, wiped the dust from the gilded tops of the pages, fingered its colored-ribbon page markers. It was a vestige from another era, and as I read the inscriptions on the front pages in my grandmother's spidery cursive—her place of baptism, her date of Holy Matrimony, her home parish in Oregon—I felt compelled to investigate.

I found not only words for communion, funerals, and ordinations but prayers for Our National Life, Our Enemies, and the Victims of Addiction. My eyes skimmed the catechism; in time, I would come to love the straightforward Q & A ("What are we by nature? *We are part of God's creation, made in the image of God;* What does it mean to be created in the image of God? *It means we are free to make choices; to love, to create, to reason, and to live in harmony with creation and with God*"), but that day in my parents' sitting room it reminded me of advice we'd been given after Blake was killed, in terms of what to tell his three-year-old son: Only answer what is asked; when he's ready to know more, he'll ask the next question. In taking for granted a belief I didn't yet feel, the approach put me off.

I continued thumbing the pages. The psalms, all 150 of them; a list of which readings belong with which days. I'd always liked having an assignment, and here was page after page of them! I happened upon Daily Devotions for Individuals and Families, moved the green ribbon to "In the Morning," and took the book home with me. Its weight in my purse felt almost like a secret, as though I'd found a photo album of my own twin, whose identity had been kept from me but which I'd always intuited.

For the next six months, in my small corner of the floor, I turned every morning to the green ribbon, opened the Prayer

Book, and spoke the words taken from Psalm 51, words I hadn't intended to memorize. But then, on that July morning, on my way to the Virginia studio for a day of work, they just came.

Give me the joy of your saving help again, and sustain me with your bountiful Spirit.

PRAYER WAS SO available, so here-and-now! I was giddy with infatuation, in love with the spaciousness it offered, the plummeting straight down, the falling without having to land. I approached the Prayer Book with the same eagerness with which I'd once waited for the sound of the station wagon's tires to thump on the carport, signaling that Mom was off to the store and I had the house to myself to look through her not-very-well-hidden copy of *The Joy of Sex*. In church, I lined up to take communion. And in it I took of the tactile (indeed, ingested) offering of love and community.

A yoga teacher used to guide us through relaxation by asking us to "invite our bellies to expand, in all dimensions, like a balloon." Now I saw what she meant. Tight chinks inside of me were expanding, as if the mortar itself could breathe, and I looked beyond the wacky notion of inviting my belly to do anything.

The tenets of the church began to bother me less. Perhaps, used to their claims, I began to filter out what seemed outlandish. Or maybe my heart opened, as I began to see that faith depends on more than rote catechism. Many people take the events of the Hebrew Bible and the gospels as literal fact; many others read them as metaphor. But metaphor is never "mere." I had a graduate degree in English, after all, as well as years of therapy; I'd staked many claims on subtext.

I still wondered, though, if the figurative angle was a huge cop-out, a gigantic loophole. I still worried, as I bit my lip during the *Agnus Dei ("Lamb of God, you take away the sins of the world")* and the singing of *"My blood is drink indeed, says the LORD,"* that I was a hypocrite to slide along on the benefits without tackling the tough stuff.

A few months before coming to Virginia, I had attended a baptism. I hadn't been to one since my brother's, some thirty years earlier. I was curious, as though tuning in to the Discovery Channel. But I vowed, with the others and "with God's help," in the words of the Prayer Book, *"To continue in the apostles' teaching and fellowship, in the breaking of bread, and in the prayers."* I felt the power of communion, not just in the bread and wine but in fellowship. "The body of Christ," I understood for the first time, wasn't "just" his resurrected form or a wheat wafer but this group of people, renewing their vows to love and serve one another.

Maybe it started with that nightmare of walking naked on Bayview Avenue, but the sensation of being watched had stuck with me, and not always unpleasantly. Exposure frightened me, yes—but as I grew older, the sensation became a kind of secret showing off, like those pretend speeches in the car. In the pool at the Brooklyn Y, when I first started swimming for fitness, I'd imagine my coworkers—the male ones, in mostly supervisory roles—seeing how neatly I sliced through the water, how cleanly I kick-turned, and saying to one another, "Wow. I didn't know she had it in her." For years after a boyfriend had told me, our first morning together, that he never would have guessed that I was so sensual, I carried his comment around like a shroud, hidden knowledge to balance out my often frosty demeanor. *They have no idea,* I'd tell myself at parties or bars when I held myself aloof. As during those impassioned speeches in front of the mirror, I didn't have to interact or give anything away. I knew who I was, and that was enough.

But now as the baby gurgled and we all grinned, I felt no self-consciousness. I felt completely connected to the people around me—strangers, most of them—and wholly without pretense or guard. I felt a part of something much, much larger and more complete than I alone could ever be, and at the same time utterly exposed as myself.

Belonging to something did not mean losing my identity—or my intelligence. At the baptismal font, the priest cupped water over the baby's head and then prayed aloud from the Rite of Baptism: *"Sustain her. Give her an inquiring and discerning heart, the courage to will and to persevere, a spirit to know and love you, and the gift of joy and wonder in all your works."*

No subtext there. The meaning was clear and forthright, as it broke over the crown of my head and ran its liquid warmth down my body. Those words, some thirty-seven years earlier, had been spoken for me. I felt acceptance, yes, and love—but even more than that. What made me weep was hearing those words *inquiring* and *discerning.* Thinking wasn't just allowed but sanctioned. I belonged, all of me.

Glory to the Father, and to the Son, and to the Holy Spirit: As it was in the beginning, is now, and will be for ever.

Mockingbirds called along the fence, and the cows lowered their thick necks to the grass. Swallows darted out of the barn and flickered toward the trees at the edge of the field.

Footsteps, running. Peter, the poet from Atlantic City, approached in his running shorts and shoes, gave a little wave as he passed. An engine, the bum-*bump* of car wheels in the pitted road: Swanny on his morning maintenance run, lifting his hand from the steering wheel of his pickup.

Not wanting to speak before eight o'clock was not new. Neither was noticing the birds, the chicory, the cows, the yellow light. What was new—what, that July morning in Virginia, I first articulated as a gift of the spirit, a benefit of prayer—was the quality of the noticing. "What a strange thing to wonder about," my mother used to say when I asked where Blackie, the swayback horse who grazed in a pasture near my school, went at night. "Can't get anything past you," my college boyfriend used to say—or, from time to time, "Jeez, Lindsey, give it up."

But now I understood that noticing, paradoxically, could mean letting go. *There go my thoughts,* I'd been told to think in Centering Prayer. *See? Another paranoia, floating right on by,* as if they were leaves on a stream and I was the bridge under which they passed. Easier said than done, of course. And yet—if only for a moment, how transforming!

When I'm in the pool, my body knows to turn and breathe, my legs to kick, my arms to pull. I can think "left arm" and articulate a better stroke, a neater angle. But after fifty laps, when I lie back and close my eyes, I lose all awareness of my body. If I think "left heel," I can't isolate it. Instead, I float—not only on the surface itself but on the sensation of floating: my weightless body, the water around my face, the quiet calm in my mind. I don't feel myself move, but when I open my eyes, my feet no longer point straight at the shallow-end wall. I have been turned on the surface of the water, the way a stick is carried by an eddy.

Prayer had confirmed the value of that bedside moment with Blake, and now it let me move past it, too. As I began to separate my sorrow over him from my own longing, I started to see ways of honoring the shrine without falling into a crypt. Prayer had shown me something larger, something as expansive as the Pacific when I'd hid in my mother's lap. There, buried in the cotton of her skirt, her strong broad hand in my hair, her tummy vibrating as she spoke with my father, I didn't have to look at that endless ocean outside the car window. I could retreat— maybe not for long ("All right," she'd say, "that's enough, you sack of potatoes," and up I'd sit)—but, usually, for long enough.

Prayer didn't offer a hiding place. There was nothing of avoidance in it. I wasn't alone, scripting my conversations to show off a side of me I kept tucked away, but alone with God—a concept I was still getting used to. What hooked me about prayer was the way in which it mandated an attention to detail. It heightened my awareness while dismantling awareness's more disturbing aspects.

In my anxiety, I'd clung to every little thing, as though the smallest incidences held deep significance. Missing three lights in a row; an impatient driver zipping past my car as I parallel-parked; a barking dog: These things could, and did, make me cry. One day, on a hike in the hills above Sonoma a few weeks before I first went to All Souls, I'd stopped on the trail and looked out over the buckeyes and the manzanita, the madrones and live oaks—trees I palmed as I passed to feel their bark, as smooth and familiar to me as my mother's arm. Except that November day, the branches of one tree spelled KILL. I never heard birds singing in Greek, but when I read *Mrs. Dalloway* that summer in Virginia, I understood how Septimus could.

Now, though, closing my eyes in prayer, I found not the constriction of taking everything personally but the amazing boundlessness of consciousness. I saw a void shot through with dots and dashes of light, untempered by time or space, as if the universe had turned itself inside out through my mouth. And when I opened my eyes, I saw my part in the whole. The chicory, the cows, the birds, the branches of the trees—all became neutral, objective, and more beautiful than ever.

I reached the door of my studio—and I am not making this up—just as I finished the prayer from Psalm 51. There was the geranium I'd planted in a coffee can. There was Dante's *Inferno,* opened to the page I'd left the day before, my limited Italian mattering not one whit next to the gorgeousness of saying aloud *"Che non sa che so faccia."* I fit the key in the lock and stepped into the room I had been given to do nothing more all day than pay attention. Thanks to prayer, I had a new way to do so.

Amen.

CHAPTER FOUR

Come to me, all you that are weary and are carrying heavy burdens, and I will give you rest. . . . For my yoke is easy, and my burden is light.

MATTHEW 11:28; 30

My nephew was born in March 1990. At that time, and for months afterward, I'd been so angry at Blake and Sheryl that I had been unable to send a baby gift, let alone to think of Dylan as separate from them. And then, on Thanksgiving night when he was eight months old, I met him. He grabbed the beads I wore around my neck and didn't let go. I have a picture of the moment, and in it we are staring at each other, foreheads touching, as if taking in all that we could not yet know.

Dylan lived with his parents in a series of apartments in San Francisco for nine months. During that time, my parents got frequent phone calls in the middle of the night, in which Sheryl said they were out of diapers or milk and Blake was nowhere to be found. Dad would get up, get dressed, go to the twenty-four-hour Walgreens, and deliver the goods. When I suggested that doing so wasn't Dad's job, Mom snapped at me that I didn't know "what it's like to have a screaming baby at 2 A.M.!" More and more, Dylan stayed at Mom and Dad's until, a month or so after my visit to the Twin Peaks apartment, he moved in for what Blake termed "temporary custody." Over the next three years, until Blake was shot, he and Sheryl showed up on Dylan's birthday, at Christmas, on unannounced afternoons to take Dylan to the zoo or the park (and, once, to visit friends of Blake's in Florida). Then they'd go AWOL, as my mother put it, for weeks on end. They broke up, got back together, and moved yet again—at one point, into a U-Haul truck on Funston Avenue, where Blake sold roses to passing cars.

After Blake's death, Sheryl would call but not come by when she'd said she would. Months would go by in which my parents would hear nothing from her. After time with her—an afternoon here and there; a Christmas visit with her family—Dylan would return troubled and anxious, petulant and clingy, sometimes even hostile, lashing out in kicks and temper tantrums. I watched him grab her ankles every time she left, and I jumped to conclusions and, yes, judgment when she didn't show up again for months. Whatever demons she battled, I saw the cost on her son, whose body racked with sobs every time she stood him up: "But *why* can't I live with Mommy?" (At four, he asked me matter-of-factly one day, "What's a mother?")

My parents struggled with being thrust into parenthood all over again, and with protecting Dylan from his mother's unreliability while supporting his need for a relationship with her. "These are supposed to be our 'golden years'!" my mother snorted one night after returning Dylan to bed the fourth time in a row. I never heard my parents speak critically of Sheryl in front of Dylan, or anyone for that matter. "She's his mother," they always reiterated. "She'll always be his mother."

Someone, though, had to step up in a formal way. My parents were already taking Dylan to the doctor, tucking him in at night, enrolling him in school, driving him to play dates. They were his parents—in fact, if not yet on paper. So, when Dylan was in kindergarten, they filed for legal guardianship. And, in March 1995, when Dylan had just turned five and had lived with Grandpa and Grandma as long as he could remember, my parents were granted custody.

GROWING UP, I'D seen my brother get away with breaking my dollhouse furniture or throwing water balloons at a neighbor's car. "I'll never do it again," he promised, and our parents replied, "All right, then." One night I listened through the bathroom wall as he slithered out of yet another consequence, and I seethed with resentment. *Someday you'll pay for this.* I was only eight, but I knew my parents were making a mistake. Later, I saw my prediction fulfilled. When I learned that Blake had stolen a credit card from my father's wallet, a week after breaking into my parents' house to steal limited-edition books, I suggested to my mother that they call the police. She gave me various excuses— Dad had canceled the card; Dad said the police were too busy to interfere with "family disputes"; Dad had arranged to get the windows rigged onto the alarm system—before her voice broke in anguish with the real reason: "Your father doesn't want to!" And now, Blake was dead—and Mom and Dad were once again picking up after him. And yet, as my mother said, what choice did they have?

My parents adored Dylan. Dad especially seemed to revel in the errands-running aspect of parenthood, cheerfully taking Dylan to school, to the store, to the hobby shop, to the ice-cream parlor. And Mom would say, "Dylan is such wonderful company. You two"—Blake and I—"were such opposites. Dylan's right in the middle." But the strain wore at them. They were in their late sixties and had already raised two children. At cocktail hour or Dylan's bedtime, they were more than happy to foist homework- and toothbrush-monitoring duty on a babysitter, the housekeeper who often stayed late, or—if I was around—me.

Since the night I met him, I'd adored my nephew. I loved spending time with him, and he brought me joy. But sometimes the ambiguity of the situation wore on me. On family vacations, Dylan played with other kids in the swimming pool, kids whose parents sat next to me and confided their parenting issues until Dylan called for me by my first name. Then the other parents, and their kids, looked at me askance. Who was this "Lindsey"?

I was aware of inhabiting a weird middle ground, playmate and (much) older sister to Dylan, as well as a third authority figure and parental peer to my own parents. One moment, my parents and I huddled to confer on the appropriate consequences after Dylan took out a rowboat without permission or told a fib. But then I'd find myself in the backseat, next to a little boy who kicked my feet and shared my M&Ms as Dad drove us home. And when I heard Dylan say, "I won't do it another time, I promise," I was listening through the bathroom wall to my brother all over again. On vacations, I always got a room of my own, but as I walked back one night, looking into the room I'd just left to see Dylan crawling into bed without having picked up his dirty swimsuit, I couldn't decide where I wanted to be. Or where I should be.

Mom would say, "He's never in as good a shape as when he's been with you." And one Sunday evening, she reported with a kind of amazement that Dylan had brought his dinner plate to the sink and announced, "This is what I do at Lindsey's."

"Go have fun," my mother told me then. "You're lucky you can."

Soon after returning home from Virginia, I'd begun to look for a new apartment in San Francisco, to be closer to my teaching job. One afternoon, Mom asked how the search was going. I said something about the high prices and single-digit vacancy rate.

"Your father will help. Just get a two-bedroom so Dylan can move in with you." And then, before I could respond, she added, "I'm kidding, you know."

Dad was more circumspect. When I'd decided, back in 1993, to leave New York and return to California for grad school, he'd sympathized with the difficulty of the decision, whereas my mother, when I admitted mixed feelings about being close to home, had burst into tears. Dad understood the weight of family burden, having left his own unhappy past in Oregon to make a life for himself in San Francisco where, he later told me, "things were happening in 1955." He'd never looked back, going to law school at night while he and my mother dated and then becoming the first associate at a posh law firm not to have graduated from Boalt, Stanford, or an Ivy League. When I talked to Dad about feeling responsible for Dylan, Dad would look serious: "You have your own life, honey. Dylan is not your responsibility."

But wasn't Dylan part of my life, just as Blake had been when he was lying and stealing and doing drugs and I was off in

New York under maternal mandate to have fun and be carefree? And didn't my nephew bring me a chance—maybe my only one— at parenthood? I was nearing forty and single. In the meantime, here was this sweet boy with his bell-like laugh and love of the Beatles, Beethoven, and fried rice. When I moved to San Francisco, he began spending Tuesday nights at my place, where I cleared space for Mr. Bubble and his toothbrush and kept his favorite Roald Dahl books. I loved those Tuesday nights, but I was always glad to have the place back to myself on Wednesdays, too.

At nine, Dylan was in the passenger seat when his babysitter drove into a tree. The air bag punched him in the face. I showed up the next day to find him staring expressionless at cartoons from the couch. "We've brought him ice cream, but all he wants to do is watch TV," my mother whispered to me in the doorway. "He hasn't said a word."

I sat next to him. I don't recall saying anything, but within a half hour, I got the whole story of the collision. "I can talk to you," he said one Tuesday night after I tucked him into bed on my futon, leaving the light and his favorite Bach cello suites on low.

And now, with Dylan in fourth grade, Mom and Dad had started looking into boarding school. They weren't happy with his school in San Francisco, and they felt increasingly overwhelmed by the day-in-day-out demands of parenting a nine-year-old boy. The prospect—for fifth grade!—seemed downright Dickensian, although I had to admit the brochures did look nice: "Our family," dropped out in tasteful type from four-color photos of autumnal New England, nurturing-looking teachers deep in discussion with eager-faced young boys and girls amid the foliage. Dylan himself was keen on the idea, seeing it as an adventure in instant siblinghood.

But *boarding school*? Was it an opportunity for Dylan, or the last chance for me? And even if I took Dylan in to live with me, did that mean that doing so was the right choice?

I wrestled with these questions one hot Friday afternoon as I drove up to Healdsburg. I was on my way to the Bishop's Ranch, a property owned by the Episcopal Diocese of California and site of many parish retreats. When I'd started attending All Souls in Berkeley, I'd seen the bulletin board with photos of smiling parishioners under the words PARISH RETREAT cut from colored construction paper; such an event had then seemed the type of wholesome activity in the name of organized religion that gave me the willies. But by September of 1999, I was looking forward to a weekend of Indian summer heat and fellowship and lots of jug wine. And, as my car lurched through Santa Rosa traffic, to clarity about Dylan.

PAMELA'S EYES HAD twinkled when I told her my new San Francisco address. "You're in the Haight!" She grinned. "You get to go to All Saints'!"

I felt at home the instant I stepped into the wood-paneled interior on Waller Street, fragrant with incense and Murphy's Oil Soap. The incense made me sneeze, but I soaked up the High Church liturgy ("smells and bells") as if it were a bubble bath: the richness of embroidered vestments and choir voices; the swinging of the thurible with its trail of smoke; the gleaming of candlelight on brass. During my first Holy Week at All Saints', the vestments stripped of color and the brass put away, the Oriental rugs rolled up and the flowers tossed, I felt as shaken as though by a physical blow. I already knew what had happened on Good Friday; now I felt it.

I became an official member of All Saints', being confirmed in the Episcopal Church at a small ceremony to which my parents, nephew, aunt (who was also my godmother), and uncle came. Living only two blocks away from All Saints', I showed up on Saturday mornings to help serve the weekly food program and on Wednesday evenings to participate in (and, soon, organize) the adult education series. And I brought Dylan with me frequently.

He'd first joined me in church when he was four. The next day, he'd lifted his sandwich bread overhead and broke it in two. Until he understood what the bread and wine signified, though, I didn't think he should partake of communion. And I wasn't sure he should drink wine, even a small sip. What did Kenneth, the priest at All Saints', think?

"Anyone with the desire to take communion understands enough," he told me.

I considered this. Wasn't the blurb on the bulletin, *"All who desire to grow in the love of God and neighbor are welcome to receive communion,"* one of the reasons I felt at home at All Saints'? And then Kenneth quoted Jesus' words about the little children coming to him. I saw the point, just as I saw how my own concern about doing the "right thing" often got in the way.

One Sunday morning at All Saints', Dylan had tapped my arm. He tapped again, more urgently, then tugged on my sleeve. I peered out from my hands, pressed against my face the way I'd seen my mother do at St. Stephen's all those years before.

"Lindsey," he whispered, loudly.

"Sh."

"Why are you crying?"

I'd watched my mother disappear when I sat by her side. Was that what Dylan saw me do now?

I turned to him. "It's okay," I whispered. "They're good tears."

I cry a lot in church, not because of any particular passage in the lessons or reference in the sermons (although that can happen too) as much as from the upswelling I feel within its walls. I can't define it narrowly as "joy" or "bliss" or "sorrow" or "love" or "gratitude"—it is somehow all emotion, unmistakable in its power and complexity. It feels beyond label, an organic experience of being, pure acknowledgment of life. The presence of God—and I was glad, that morning as many since, to share it with my nephew.

And yet, despite that release, I rarely prayed in church. I stood with everyone else during the Prayers of the People and spoke the words of the Nicene Creed, the words that had given me such pause during my first visit to All Souls in Berkeley. A beautiful and real power always washes over me as I sit in the congregation, whether the church is full of people or sparsely attended, and as I line up to take communion. Back in the pew, I put my face in my hands and listen to the priests repeat *"The body of Christ, the bread of heaven"* over and over at the altar rail. It feels holy, yes, and it sustains me. But the prayer that transports me out of my body and changes my life? In those days, I'd rarely experienced that in church.

But I had in nature. That was one reason I was on my way to the All Saints' retreat, after all. Prayer would answer my questions, I told myself as I took the Healdsburg exit off Highway 101. It had to.

THE NEXT AFTERNOON, at the Bishop's Ranch, I sat outside on a bench beneath a grape arbor and asked God to help me figure out the right thing to do. It was the second day of the retreat, a time so far full of jokes and raised voices and wine. A fat bee buzzed my shoulder, and thick woody cords of wisteria twisted through the arbor, tangling with vines from which bitter grapes hung. Limp leaves cast green upon the pebbled path, a green so saturated it might have been pureed grass.

"Something out of a Merchant Ivory production, isn't it?" I asked as Kenneth sat down next to me. "You know, the shady bower, perfect for secrets."

He gave a slight chuckle, and I felt silly, caught making light of the very thing I longed for: huddled confidences and revelation. And worse, pretentious, for dropping highbrow allusions. Just steps away, inside the ranch house, the rest of the All Saints' group chatted and laughed, but outside, I felt the pressure of incipient confession. Now was my chance—if I made a good case, he might help me.

I explained the boarding school prospect. Kenneth nodded. "It's hard to feel responsible when you have no control," he said. "Your parents are his guardians. You can still be involved in the decision, perhaps by researching schools, or by planning activities you and he can continue doing together."

This made sense, but it didn't quite address the tangle I felt inside.

"You know," I said, "the truth is, I feel stuck. Everything is so fraught in San Francisco. Even the view outside my window. Especially the view outside my window." I gave what I hoped was a wry, insouciant smile. I didn't want to be a downer, what my mother would have termed "too heavy." But my reference had been oblique. Kenneth had no way of knowing what the view meant to me.

The quality of light was the first thing I'd noticed when

I'd walked in my new one-bedroom. Unobstructed northern view. Angel Island. The Headlands. Belvedere Island. The Golden Gate Bridge. It was the nicest place I'd seen in weeks of looking, and I wasn't going to turn it down because of the view, but doing so crossed my mind.

I'd moved to New York when I was twenty-three for the reason many twenty-three-year-olds move to New York. I'd stayed for nine years because I loved it. I loved the seasons and the people and the energy and anonymity of a city whose very skyline radiated potential. Walking up Fifth Avenue at eight A.M., when the sidewalks were clotted with people on our way to work, and then home through the Village on cobblestones glowing pink from sunsets over the Hudson River, I felt gloriously free. In New York, no one knew or would have particularly cared that my mother's architect uncle had designed San Francisco's Castro Theatre and Oakland's Paramount. Or that my brother had once charged tourists in Tiburon five dollars to watch him catch leopard sharks from the Bay, and, at thirteen, motored alone across some of the nation's biggest shipping lanes in a Boston Whaler to visit me at my freshman boardinghouse in Berkeley. The Golden Gate Bridge was a world-famous landmark, but in New York, I didn't have to look at it and be reminded of my brother climbing its north tower.

These associations weren't pejorative, or even particularly downbeat, but they were laden. In New York, I could define myself as independent, at least externally, from family. I could walk its streets and not be reminded of my brother's daredevilishness and my mother's boastfulness, often so entangled. And now I was back in San Francisco, staring at the Golden Gate Bridge and worrying, once again, about my role in my family.

But Kenneth didn't know all that. He didn't smile, either. He just watched me, his gaze piercing with concern as his jaw clenched and unclenched as though reacting to too-cold ice cream. Such scrutiny made me uncomfortable, and I felt relieved when he glanced at his watch. "I need to get back inside," he said, "but I do have a suggestion."

I felt hope: *He's going to tell me the right thing to do.*

"You might try praying the prayer of Dame Julian, the one we use with the rosary on Tuesday nights."

I'd been to the Tuesday evening service. I'd passed an Anglican rosary through my fingers while reciting, *"All shall be well and all shall be well and all manner of thing shall be well. . . ."* I had no problem with the words. Attributed to Dame Julian of Norwich, a fourteenth-century anchoress, the words are lovely. They just didn't seem to fit the bill.

"You may find that helps." He pressed my hand between his own, damp palms. "I'll keep you in my prayers."

I nodded, blinking, as he walked off. That was it?

The chapel bell rang to mark the hour. Clearly, I decided, I wasn't spiritually evolved enough. I'd been praying for years and still didn't get it. Julian, after all, had lived through the Plague, seeing many of her townspeople and family wiped out. Those words that seemed so meager to me had been enough for her.

Was I that selfish? What kind of devotee was I? I needed to return to Go, start from scratch with this whole prayer thing. I'd been at it all wrong. Dread draped its lead apron over my shoulders.

I flashed on a gospel passage that had always stymied me: *"Come to me, all you that are weary and are carrying heavy burdens,"* Jesus says in the eleventh chapter of Matthew's gospel, *"and I will give you rest. For my yoke is easy and my burden is light."*

I love the open-endedness of the Episcopal Church and its embrace of what the postcommunion prayer refers to as "these holy mysteries," but I crave the details. Just how, exactly, do you put down a heavy burden and pick up an easy yoke when both are figures of speech—and, in this case, representative (it seemed) of the same thing? How do you tell them apart? Scripture is all over the place on family duty, so I couldn't find a clear answer there. And then there was the whole notion of each of us having a cross to bear. If it's a real cross—that is, a burden—then how can it be easy and light? After all, there was nothing light and easy about the Passion.

Okay, I told myself, *you're overthinking.* I felt doomed as the perennial outsider, left to peer in from the cold at the true believers basking in cozy assurance.

I stood up from the bench and walked past the ranch house, ducking beneath the windows so I wouldn't be seen playing hooky. I headed out the gate at the edge of the parking lot and up the trail through the dry hills. I walked a mile with my head down, watching for rattlesnakes, and stopped at the top of a rise to catch my breath.

In my time at All Saints', I'd become familiar with the New Zealand Prayer Book's version of the Lord's Prayer, arrived at by translating the English prayer book into Maori and then back again into English. In that way, the request to *"Forgive us our trespasses, as we forgive those who trespass against us"* becomes, *"For the hurts we absorb from one another, forgive us."* This made a lot more sense than thinking of NO TRESPASSING signs that I'd once ignored without peril.

I imagined a bundle at my feet, lumpy and heavy. I didn't want to throw away my family, but maybe I could toss the burden of feeling so tortured and responsible? I looked around to make sure no one could see, and then I bent to pick up my imaginary bundle. "Here." The sound of my voice was lost in the hot air on top of that hillside. I spoke louder. "Here!" I tossed it down the hill, past the oaks and toward the narrow ribbon of the Russian River, where it would wind among the vineyards and redwoods on its way out to sea. *Take it away.*

Okay, I thought. That miraculous release should be coming along any minute now.

I lifted my face to the sun, to the relentless blue sky, empty of softening cloud or haze. I closed my eyes and felt the sun's heat as warmth on and into my body. A breeze stirred the dry grass.

I love you.

I opened my eyes. The voice had been clear—not particularly loud, but unmistakably precise. I turned around. Dry grass, a circle of oak trees, a path down toward the road. No one.

I drank syrup once. At a party in high school, after smoking pot with my friends, I made my way into the kitchen, where I rummaged the cupboards until I found a bottle of Log Cabin. I poured a tablespoon of the stuff, lifted it like cough medicine to my lips, drank. A girl from English class gave me a dirty look, but I didn't care. The syrup was just what I'd craved, and more: Sweet and thick and viscous against my parched throat, it spread throughout my chest. *At last.* Pamela, that first day we talked, had compared God's love to a shaft of sunlight. I felt it now as syrup. Every tension in my body released, as though I might slide into the dry warm earth.

Then the sensation vanished, and I was terrified.

BACK HOME FROM the retreat, I took Kenneth's advice. I'd been introduced to the Anglican rosary by an All Saints' parishioner who made them from pretty beads, rose quartz and cobalt glass and light-as-a-feather bone. I liked the neat division of beads into seven days, four cruciform beads, one invitatory bead, one crucifix, and all the meaning those numbers signified. (With thirty-three beads—another symbolic number, that of Jesus' age when he was crucified—the Anglican rosary is shorter than the Roman Catholic one, and it doesn't have a prescribed script.)

Now I made my own rosary from beads I bought on Haight Street, and I sent away for a pamphlet, *Praying the Anglican Rosary.* I ran through the rosary every morning, repeating Dame Julian's prayer but also creating my own by the simple repetition of any three phrases. Sometimes I borrowed from a psalm, sometimes I said what came to mind. "The wind in the trees," I offered up one morning ninety-nine times, until my breath and the wind felt one.

I'd begun praying with the simplest of words—*Help* and *I hurt,* pleas that, like toads and worms in a fairy tale, had needed to get out of my mouth. But the words themselves mattered less than the saying of them. *All shall be well,* like *I am here, you are here,* like *Help,* provided a miner's lamp, a path, a voice for the ineffable. A way in.

I could start praying the rosary as soon as my coffee was ready, and after three rounds, I knew I had finished. Sometimes, it seemed I'd never get through and other days, my thumb would bump into the last bead with the shock of a time warp: Already? With the rosary, I literally had something to hold on to. All my needs—for a prop, for a script, for a time limit—were answered by the primal, basic action of moving beads in my hand. Some days, I carried my rosary with me, tucked in my pocket, where the very touch of the beads felt like prayer enough. Other times, I prayed the rosary as I drove, moving the beads in one hand while steering with the other.

The desire for prayer had always felt urgent and pure. Unlike the compulsion to get it right, which came from somewhere else—the scolding voice of my kindergarten teacher, perhaps, or my own fear that if I didn't play by the rules, I'd be tossed out of the game. As I held the smooth glass beads in my fingers, I saw once again: There is no one "right" way to pray.

I began to untangle "should" from "want"—and to understand "want" for the first time, not only as selfishness (or even desire) but as yearning. That day in Healdsburg, I'd longed for succor but didn't know how to be honest, to come right out and ask for it. I couldn't expect Kenneth to read my thoughts, even if he was a priest. And yet he had seen through my attempts to hide my concern. He had gripped my hand. He had listened. Maybe my real feelings weren't such a downer. Up on that hillside, I *had* been completely honest. I had believed myself alone there, and God had reminded me that I wasn't.

I got the message. Again. Prayer worked when I told the truth. Not when I was trying to impress, or be a good girl (or a good Episcopalian), or do things the "right way," but when I was myself. Maybe this was the way of true learning: not a thunderbolt instant but the steady accrual of experience, the way my mother and I had said those Spanish vocabulary words again and again until I had them down.

I called Kenneth to thank him for our talk and to tell him it had helped, although not at first in the way I'd wanted. This was easier to say over the phone than it would have been in person. We chatted a bit and I found myself telling him about the voice on the hillside, the voice that had said "I love you" and filled me with bliss, if only for a second.

"It scared me," I said. "It felt like God's voice. It had to be, right? But how can a God of love fill me with fear? How can an unambiguous statement of love make me so scared?"

"Oh, my dear girl," he said. "How can it not?"

WATER, WHEN WE dive into it, collapses from our weight. We plummet straight through. Yet when we lean back to float, it holds us. I had come to settle on prayer, to float on its dense, impenetrable heft. I had stopped grasping for proof, and I had found assurance.

"You're lucky," a friend had told me a few days after Blake was killed. "You have a piece of him in his son." But Dylan has never looked like Blake. He has his mother's shape of eye, her set of mouth. He takes after, more and more, his maternal grandmother. Like Blake, he has a quick intelligence, a sharp sense of humor, a tendency to tooth decay, an ability to put people at ease. He and I share goofy jokes and, yes, nicknames that no one else finds particularly amusing. As a baby, Dylan stared at me, watching my every move just as Blake had—but Dylan's eyes are blue like mine and my parents', whereas Blake's were brown, indisguisable evidence that, genetically at least, he didn't fit. In high school, Blake blared the Dead Kennedys and sported Doc Martens; the teenaged Dylan springs his savings on the collected CDs of Mozart and wears a necktie every chance he gets.

The main reason I don't see my brother in my nephew, though, has nothing to do with clothing or physical traits or sensibility.

The main reason is that I don't want to. Blake occupies a place within me that became enshrined the moment I named him. My love for Dylan is no less, just because he doesn't occupy that shrine. No one else could.

And yet, I saw as I kept praying the words of Dame Julian, in that fierce attachment to Blake, I was losing sight of what—or who—was right in front of me. Just because I lost my brother didn't mean I was going to lose Dylan. Dylan *wasn't* Blake, and "saving" Dylan wouldn't bring Blake back. I didn't know exactly how "all manner of thing" would be well, but maybe I didn't need to. In the time it took to repeat *"All shall be well, all shall be well, and all manner of thing shall be well"* eighty-four times, all manner of thing *was* well. Suspended in prayer, I had no other obligation than to breathe and move the beads through my fingers. And when I surfaced into my day, I began to see—and believe—that there was more than one right thing to do. And maybe, in my way, I was already doing some of them. After all, Dylan had brought much that was well into my life.

He'd never struggled to define my role, either. In fact, as he showed one day in the post office when he was about six, he knew who I was. I was paying for stamps when he reached for a candy cane from the cup on the counter.

"Go ahead, honey," the postal worker said, "if it's okay with your mom."

"She's not my mom."

"Oh!" The woman and I looked at him, at his steady blue eyes, his nonplussed straightforward gaze. Her face flickered in embarrassment, or alarm, and then relaxed as I nodded and he turned away from the counter, candy in hand, announcing, "She's Lindsey."

CHAPTER FIVE

We beseech you to hear us, good LORD

LITANY AT THE TIME OF DEATH,

BOOK OF COMMON PRAYER

I was balancing my checkbook on Quicken when the phone rang. I picked up on the first ring. Mom had been to a doctor about the sudden, large lump on her neck. Months later, I found the scrap of paper on which I'd written some of the words she spoke that afternoon. I'd inked them over and over in a neat, almost childlike print, as though with each impression I might make sense of their meaning. *Liver. Lungs. Lymph.*

My mother had cancer. A sentence, simple enough, that until that afternoon—April 7, 2000—I couldn't have imagined. Until that afternoon, I couldn't have put the words *cancer* and *mother* in the same sentence.

I phoned my friends Leslie and Linda, and then Dr. B. up in Davis. A friend from grad school. Voice mail, everywhere voice mail. I did not leave messages. I had the wild thought to pick up the phone book and pick a number, any number, call it, and announce,

"My mother has cancer." Then I'd know. Either the spell would be broken and I'd laugh in giddy relief, or the sentence would be real.

The fifth call reached a college friend who'd lost her own mother a few years earlier. "Make every moment count," she said. "Spend every minute you can with her."

That wasn't what I wanted to hear. I was still making sense of simple arithmetic—my mother has cancer—and my friend was talking higher calculus. I was still absorbing diagnosis. I wasn't ready for prognosis. My mother wasn't going to die. I didn't need to worry about "every moment." I mumbled something, hung up, and walked out the door.

By the time I reached my car, parked at the top of Ashbury Street, I was gulping air. I couldn't break down yet. I had to get across town. I unlocked the door and got in, turned the ignition. Through the windshield, the city spread north toward my parents' neighborhood and the bay beyond. I couldn't imagine getting across town.

"Oh, my God," I said. "Are we ever going to need you now."

I pulled the car away from the curb and headed downhill. It was a sunny, cool day.

FOR THE NEXT six months, I had a job to do. My mother had stage IV non-small cell lung cancer. After her first chemo, I phoned relatives and friends from my cubicle at a magazine where I freelanced to announce that she felt fine and wanted leg of lamb for dinner. I cooked rich risottos and creamy soups, foods she'd never chosen before. ("Oh, just sherbet for me," she'd say on family outings to Shaw's, the ice cream parlor where Dad ordered marble fudge, Blake went for rocky road, and I always had thin mint.) I stayed with her when Dad went out of town, and I moved Dylan in with me for three weeks so that she and Dad could stay in Sonoma between treatments. I took Dylan to summer camp. He'd been accepted and chosen to go to boarding school before Mom got her diagnosis, and we moved forward with this plan. We all operated under one assumption, one my mother told me the afternoon of April 7 when I arrived and she took me in her arms: "I'm going to beat this thing." So I took Dylan shopping for clothes for his new school, and I helped get him packed. I went to all of my mother's oncology appointments, even when she asked, "Don't you have to be at the magazine?" I took notes and asked questions that made her roll her eyes and, later, turn to me: "What was it Dr. Smith said about waiting before eating?" I shelved my novel and spent my time at the keyboard researching cancer treatments and writing long daily entries in a file called Write It All Down, after what my friend Michael had said when I told him the news.

I did these things not out of obligation but because I wanted to. They gave me not only purpose but a kind of pleasure.

"What's wrong with me?" I asked Dr. B. "My mother has cancer and I actually feel good."

"You are doing something with enormous meaning."

"My mother is dying."

"Exactly."

For it soon became clear, despite her vow to "beat this thing," that she was dying. After our initial euphoria when a CT scan showed 90 percent of the tumor gone, we got the news that, in the two weeks between treatments, the tumor had returned big as ever. She'd need a constant drip to keep the tumor at bay. No one—not even my mother—could withstand that.

"Why is the medicine making her feel so bad?" Dylan asked. "Isn't the medicine supposed to make her better?"

I explained the logic of chemotherapy and radiation.

"So why can't they just cut out the bad parts?"

I drew a stick figure, circling the approximate locations of the liver, lungs, lymph, and thoracic spine.

"It's everywhere," he said.

At the end, it went into her brain. The radiation oncologist admired and liked my mother so much, she told me on the phone, that she hadn't been able to tell Mom. So she was telling me.

I hung up the phone. I screamed. "Don't you dare do this to her!"

There wasn't anybody else in my kitchen, but I knew whom I was yelling at.

God, like prayer, was no longer an abstraction. We'd moved beyond the awkward politesse of a first date and were in a committed relationship. God could see me in fear and worry and out-and-out terror. I was furious at God. And in that moment I didn't care what God thought.

WHEN I WAS a girl, my mother's voice, exclamatory in joy, dismay, and surprise, punctuated my consciousness from the moment she sang out "Good morning!" as she snapped up my window shades, to the moment she closed my door with "Sleep tight, honey. Tomorrow's another day." Her enthusiasms were effusive, and her disappointments trailed overhead like the rain cloud in the *Addams Family* cartoon. Whether soothing my fevered brow or squashing a spider (one swoop of her big-boned hand, a crunch of paper towel, and *there,* the bug was dead), she was indomitable, a force of life.

From her message that I had "no reason to be tired," I learned to keep my insecurities and longings to myself. Mom went through my Wizard of Oz trash can to dig out my childhood drawings and stories, she later told me, "to find out what you were thinking."

"Why didn't you just ask me?"

"Oh, I don't like to pry."

When I was fifteen and high on painkillers from having my wisdom teeth removed, I showed her my high school yearbook, including the pictures of my current crush. The following day, I heard her on the phone with one of her friends: "Some boy named Chris! You should see his hair!"

My mother taught me to dress—skirt, pressed blouse, leather shoes, purse—for church, for lunches downtown, and for airplane travel ("After all," she'd say, "you'll be arriving somewhere"). When taking off my wristwatch in the evenings, whether or not I'm going out, I hear her voice with its touch of amused irony: "Ladies don't need to know the hour after dark." She cared about appearances, but dismissed what other people thought. Unless she loved them, and then they could wound her to the quick. Growing up, I'd heard her break into sobs after coming home from a dinner party at her perception that Dad, in his characteristic brusqueness, had offended one of her friends. "Oh, for Christ's sake!" my dad would yell. "You're so oversensitive!"

My depression had wounded her. When I'd admitted that I'd thought of suicide, she'd wailed. "How do you think that makes me feel?"

"You know, Mom, this isn't about you." She couldn't accept that, not from me.

Cancer, it is said, acts like a refining fire. It reduces people—not in the sense of physical diminishment (although my always-hardy mother became frail) but in the way of a sauce over heat. When my mother was eighteen, she caught tuberculosis from her best friend and dropped out of college to spend nine months in the hospital. She never went back to UC Berkeley, or any other college, although she'd had a 4.0 in her first semester. Why not, I once asked her, and she looked at me as though I'd asked why not chew with my mouth open. The answer was obvious: It wasn't the thing to do. Her friends had moved on, getting pinned and engaged and married, while Mom continued making weekly trips to the hospital to spit into paper cups and have tubes snaked into her lungs. By the time she was well enough to move out of her parents' house, she got a job and a roommate and lived the single life in San Francisco until she met my father when she was twenty-eight.

My mother never admitted regret at not finishing college. She didn't believe in regret. Instead, her voice mingling accusation and longing, she used to say, "I don't have the education you do." Mom believed in moving forward, not looking back, and certainly not "dwelling." What's done is done, she'd say. She distrusted hovering concern, loathed wringing hands and worry. I learned early on that the worst four-letter word of all, the word to avoid at all cost—not just in its uttering but in its very concept— was *pity*. She didn't want any, and—she'd announce firmly, in case you had any doubt—she wasn't going to pass out any, either.

I was confused. Was pity so different from empathy, from compassion, from the understanding that my stomachache might indicate, if not dysentery, than the equally real desire to avoid the humiliation of Nation Ball? "Off you go," she'd say, hand pressed between my shoulder blades. No one, she frequently reminded me, ever said life was easy.

During the six months my mother fought cancer, she didn't want anyone feeling sorry for her, and she hated the helplessness that her body manifested. And yet she became warmer, more effusive, more generous. "Come sit with me, darling," she'd say. Once, she had pushed me away when I tried to comfort her after she and my father had argued ("Let me be," she said. "Just let me be"), but now she told me I was her strength.

"I can't do this without you," she told me. "I'm sorry. I can't be strong for you. I have to lean on you."

"Of course, Momma, of course."

After surgery removed cancer from between her T4 and T5 vertebrae and she couldn't stand, let alone walk, I lifted her from bed to commode to wheelchair.

"Lindsey," she'd say, waving away my father or a home-care attendant with an impatient hand. "Let Lindsey do it."

She grasped my hand for hours. I'd start to gently retract it, thinking she'd fallen asleep, and her hold would spring back into a wakeful clasp. "I'll be right back, Momma," I said, and if she was alert, she'd smile and nod. *Go do what you need to do,* she seemed to say, *but come right back.*

My existence became intensified, too. The extraneous fell away, the core burned more brightly. I dropped contact with people who'd never meant very much. When one friend suggested I lock up the silver after I described trying to find a home-care attendant my mom would tolerate, when another insisted that standard procedure would put Mom on antidepressants, I stopped going to those friends for support. I confided in other friends and in people I barely knew, people who didn't tell me they understood—when, from where I sat, they had no idea. When my mother complained about the daily phone calls from her sister, whom my father called the Voice of Doom because of her hushed tone of palpable worry, I asked my aunt not to call every day to see how Mom was feeling. I spent most of my time with my family, and I didn't begrudge a minute of it. Alone, I rarely felt lonely. I cleaned like a fiend.

One day, when my mother could still walk, we stood in the shallow end of the Sonoma pool. She'd just told me how when she first came down with TB, her mother sent her to a chiropractor.

"My God," I said. "A chiropractor? For *tuberculosis?*"

"Oh, I've told you that before," she said, patting the surface of the water with her hands as if to smooth it down.

"No, Mom, you haven't. And whenever you say that you've told me something before, you haven't."

"Oh." She leaned back against the steps and kicked her legs. "Aren't you funny."

That's where, all my life up to that moment, she would have stopped. She would've changed the subject—to the pool filter needing emptying or the zinnias looking thirsty or what sounded good for dinner. But that day she kept going, talking about her mother's zany ideas on health as well as her prejudices, about my uncle's elopement and my other uncle's lifelong resentment of his wife, who, everyone knew, was smarter than he.

We talked about my father's inability to discipline Blake, and now Dylan. "You'll have a battle on your hands," she said one day. "Thank God you'll be there. You can do it. You'll have to."

We looked at each other. Her eyes were calm, wise, faraway. That was the first time I heard my mother acknowledge that she wouldn't always be around. We changed the subject.

From my perspective, my mother became more gentle, less territorial—and she would have said the same about me.

Whereas once I had pretended not to know what she was talking about when she asked about "your friend, Sharon isn't it, who works in Hollywood and married the boy from New York?" ("Who?" I asked, knowing full well she meant Susan, living in LA and a journalist in her own right), now I told her I was scared I'd never fall in love and would wind up a weirdo who lived alone with my prejudices and foibles and too many cats.

"No, you won't," she said.

One afternoon, in a fit of dusting, I propped a mirror against the wall, where it fell and cracked. Later, on the phone, I mentioned it to her.

"Star Glass," she said. "On Pacific. They'll replace it."

"Seven years' bad luck," I said.

My mother had taught me to make a wish when eating the first fruit of the season, to toss salt over my shoulder after spilling it, to give a penny with a pair of scissors, to say "Bread and butter" if I passed on the other side of a pole or hydrant from the person I was walking with. She was not a fearful person—a friend from New York still recalls her nonchalance as Dylan, then a toddler, played near the swimming pool—and yet she loved her old wives' tales.

But now she said, "No."

"What do you mean, Mom? I broke a mirror."

"No," she repeated. "No seven years' bad luck. Not for you. I won't allow it."

I could have taken her words that summer as a mother's reassurance and comfort. And surely, in part, they were. But, as I'd told a playmate when I was four, "My mommy never lies." My mother passed on her mother's superstitions and a few of her prejudices, yes—but she believed that you made your own life. And if she spoke it, it was law.

The world without my mother, as I began to consider such a prospect, seemed as foreign and unfathomable as the world without the sun or moon in it, as the words "my mother has cancer" had once been. In fact, it wasn't until two years after her death, when I went on a bicycle tour of the Southwest, that I found the right comparison. I'd been cycling all day, close to sixty miles, and it was sunset as I walked to the edge of the south rim of the Grand Canyon. I began to cry. "Finally," I said to the person next to me. "Something as big as my mother's death."

I NO LONGER had time for saying the rosary but carried it everywhere, until it broke, and then I carried the loose beads and frayed thread and tarnished cross in my pocket. In bed at night, before I fell asleep, I said a prayer from Compline: *"Keep watch, dear* LORD, *with those who work, or watch, or weep this night, and give your angels charge over those who sleep. Tend the sick, Lord Christ; give rest to the weary, bless the dying, soothe the suffering, pity the afflicted, shield the joyous; and all for your love's sake. Amen."*

One afternoon a few days before she died, I leaned over my mother, who seemed to be dozing. *"The* LORD *is my shepherd,"* I whispered.

Her eyes opened.

"I shall not want," I continued.

She frowned. "Why are you saying that?" By now, the tumor was pressing on her voice box, but her whisper was fierce—and her gaze as keen as the night I walked wet-haired into the living room, holding my boyfriend's hand, after making out in the hot tub. "Can't get anything past Mom," Blake used to say. Now, she looked irritated as well. *I haven't died yet.*

She was right. I'd begun uttering the Twenty-third Psalm not out of spontaneous emotion but as a conscious decision. *My mother is dying. Now would be an appropriate time for the Twenty-third Psalm.* She saw right through me. She could always spot a false note, however well intentioned.

The most powerful moments came, it turned out, not in words at all. They came in moments not of structure or thought but of discovery. Sitting with her as we sipped fruit smoothies and felt the sun on our skin. Watching the clouds move across the sky and thinking of the story of Creation, when God, at the end of each of the six days, said, "It is very good." What sustained me came from being with her, from looking at what I couldn't bear to see and seeing anyway. Prayer had taught me to pay attention, and during my mother's illness, I paid a lot of attention. That brought me closer to her, and closer to God.

MOM HADN'T BEEN particularly interested in the details of my return to church. When I'd told her I was going regularly to All Souls, she'd reminded me that at age four I'd responded to her description of the resurrection by saying, "Maybe someone in our family will do that." And when I'd recounted my first Maundy Thursday liturgy of the foot-washing, she had shuddered: "Someone touching my bare feet! I wouldn't like that one bit."

But to me that was the whole point. The Maundy (from the Old French for *mandate,* or *commandment,* after Jesus' new commandment to "Love one another as I have loved you"), as we celebrated it at All Saints', had moved me so much I had wept. I wanted to describe the intimacy and love I'd felt as Kenneth had sponged and toweled my bare feet. At her tone, however, and the slight downward turn of her mouth, I changed tack, retreated away from my personal account and into a recounting of the tradition that Jesus had started by washing the feet of his disciples.

"Well." She sniffed. "I don't remember all that from Sunday school."

In that way, she silenced me. And how often I wished to silence her! Over and over, when she talked about my brother climbing out of his crib at nine months or scaling the north tower of the Golden Gate Bridge at sixteen. When she stood next to me in line to have books signed by Sue Miller or Joan Didion and put her hand on my arm to announce, loudly enough for everyone on line to hear, "My daughter writes, too!" And especially when the topic turned, as it did during lunch one warm day in Sonoma before she got sick, to the river.

The Russian River, where she spent all her summers as a child and teenager, where boys called to her from the driveway and she and her friend Jackie tanned their hands by lifting them overhead as they sunbathed. I knew about Mom's victory garden, tended during the war, and the drive up Old Highway 101, when her German-born grandmothers chatted in the backseat and called each other Mrs. Pflueger and Mrs. Kauck, despite having four grandchildren in common, and where, one year, Mom dropped her doll at a corner in Petaluma that I still refer to as Where Phyllis Fell.

Now, as we both reached for a slice of tomato, she said, apropos of nothing in particular, "I'll never forget that night on the river."

Here we go, I thought, swatting away a yellow jacket from the cold cuts.

She went on to describe lying awake on the sleeping porch of her family's house one night in 1940. She was ten years old and wide awake, staring at the stars. *Who am I?*, she thought. *And how do I belong in all that?*

Her voice throbbed with intensity and her face shone rapt with the divulgence of self. I had to look away. As I had many times before, I pretended I wasn't really listening. I reached for another tomato.

I knew what the Russian River meant to her. And I, too, had glimpsed the mystery. But I didn't want to hear her talk about it, any more than she'd wanted to hear me talk about getting my bare feet touched by a priest. What, out of self-protection, had we kept from each other? What, if she hadn't gotten sick, would we still be keeping?

"MY MOTHER'S CANCER is everywhere," I told Amelia, a deacon at All Saints', who was preparing Dylan for his baptism in August. She'd come to talk to him at my apartment one Tuesday, and now that the lesson was done and Dylan had moved into the living room to watch *Arthur,* Amelia and I sat in the kitchen while water boiled for tea. "The doctor says she won't make it past the end of the year."

I'd first seen the Priestly Response in Pamela's office when I told her I didn't believe in sin. I'd recognized it when talking to Kenneth that day in the grape arbor at the Bishop's Ranch. Now it appeared on Amelia's face. She looked me steadily in the eyes, nodded, and said nothing.

"How can God let her die?" I poured Amelia a cup. "I mean, I know everyone dies, and every daughter thinks her own mother deserves special intervention, but come on!"

Amelia kept looking at me.

"Mom doesn't want to die. She's fighting as hard as she can. She wants to live. She loves life."

Amelia blew on the surface of her tea, took a sip. I had to fill the silence, I had to keep making my case, I had to get an answer.

"My dad will be lost without her. And Dylan . . . I'm fully grown, I'm an adult, but he's only ten and already lost so much. And we're all praying! What good is prayer if it isn't answered?"

I turned to put the pot back on the stove. *Keep moving,* an impulse told me. *Keep doing.* But still Amelia watched me, and so I sat down. And then she spoke.

"God does not interfere with natural processes. Hurricanes, earthquakes, tornadoes, cancer . . . these are natural processes, however destructive," she said—just like the blooming of the cherry trees every February or the birth of a child. And although God created these natural processes, she explained, God doesn't get in their way, any more than God makes the sun come out just because we're going on a picnic."

"Or make our team win," I said.

"That's right."

But God does pick favorites, I thought, *time and again.* In the Hebrew Bible and throughout the gospels, the Red Sky parts, the sky turns dark at noon, the dead are raised. "I thought God was supposed to be able to do anything. I thought prayer was supposed to work miracles."

"What God is able to do and what God does are not always the same thing," Amelia said. "What God does do is be with us through it all, no matter what happens."

This made sense, rationally. I could keep arguing the point, or I could accept some larger—and truer—meaning. But I wasn't ready to.

The following Sunday, as I approached the All Saints' altar rail for healing for my mother, I was utterly stymied. Typically, I rehearsed my supplication ahead of time. But how do you ask God to remove cancer from the lung, the liver, the lymph, the spinal column, the hip, the brain?

Amelia stopped in front of me, the little pot of chrism in her hand.

"You know," I said, my vision swimming.

Amelia took a deep breath, put her hands on my head, pressed the oil onto my forehead. "Words fail us, O Lord."

Tears spilled at my feet. My head felt liquid, full to bursting, no room for anything else besides the enormity of her implication: You don't.

UNTIL THE VERY end, my mother insisted on getting out of bed and dressed every morning, on sitting up to eat, like a civilized person. She reached hungrily for the pills I fed her, and spooned up whole-milk yogurt. Sometimes, though, I'd catch a glimpse of her as her chin nodded down onto her chest, the spoon halfway to her mouth as though it held a spadeful of wet cement. That's how I found her when I walked into the kitchen after flying back east to bring Dylan home from boarding school. "It's time," Dr. Smith had said. "Gather everyone who needs to be there."

"Look, Betty!" Dad announced, shepherding Dylan toward her. "Look who's here!"

She looked up, puzzled and irritated (she hated having visitors when she was tired, and she was too tired to put on a face that wouldn't scare Dylan with the truth). And then her voice slid from the question of who she'd hoped all day would come into the certainty of who stood in front of her: "Lindsey!"

The next morning, my father and I huddled in the kitchen. "I just can't bear to tell her." He wiped his eyes. "It breaks my heart."

"She needs to know, Dad. She deserves to know what Dr. Smith says."

Now my father waved his hand, as though to swat away that piece of information.

I pushed through the swinging door into the dining room. Mom sat in her wheelchair, staring out the window. I went over to her, and she turned and smiled.

"I talked to Dr. Smith."

"Oh?"

"Yes, Momma." Tears slid down my cheeks. "All the sleeping you've been doing, he says that's to be expected."

She peered at me. "Oh."

We'd been to Dr. Smith only a week before, and he'd said she might make it another three months. She'd asked how she would know when the end was near. She'd sleep a lot, he said.

"He says a couple of days, Mommy." I was sobbing, and our eyes did not leave each other's. "I don't know what we'll do, Mommy. But we'll be all right. I don't want you to worry. We'll be okay."

She pulled my head to her, and I breathed in the aroma of her skin, the presence that had been my earliest experience of this world. "Oh, my daughter," she whispered. "My wonderful daughter."

DYLAN SPENT HIS first days home under the dining room table, which we'd pushed into the corner to make room for Mom's hospital bed. His fifth-grade class was studying U.S. geography, and he spent his days coloring in the states on a map. Then he started making baking-soda volcanoes, and I went with him out on the deck to watch them erupt.

"Grandma looks so old," he told me one day as I folded sheets, warm from the dryer. "She didn't look that old when I left for school."

"I know."

When he asked, three or four times a day, "Why are you crying?", I always gave the same answer. "Because Grandma is dying, sweetie."

He tired of the map and the eruptions and moved upstairs to the couch, where he lay all day and watched Nickelodeon. "I'm not crying right now," he announced when I brought him a snack one afternoon, "but when she dies, I'm going to make Lake Michigan."

I had moved into my parents' house and was sleeping on Dylan's bottom bunk. I went out only to swim or run to the store. I spent my days sitting with my mother. Dylan kept telling me he had something to show me outside, and I kept telling him to wait.

Amelia stopped by one afternoon. "What image do you have of your mother healthy?" she asked me as we sat in armchairs across from Mom's bed. Mom was asleep.

I raised my arms and spread them, like a child doing *This much*. "Holding out her arms to greet me."

We talked some more, and then we approached Mom's bedside. Amelia took her hand, and Mom opened her eyes and gave a smile.

"I thought we might pray, Betty," Amelia said.

"I'd like that," my mother whispered.

"Oh, God," Amelia said, "Open wide your arms to receive Betty, a child of your own creation, a lamb of your own flock, to welcome her home with you into your everlasting love."

My mother's eyes were closed, and her face was calm and peaceful.

I looked at Amelia in panic. What was she doing?

No! I prayed. *Not yet. You can't take her. I'm not ready. I'll never be ready.*

I'D HAD A premonition. "October 26" had flashed in my mind as I stood to get our bags from the overhead compartment of the plane that had brought Dylan and me back to SFO and discovered my rosary had broken in my pocket.

Eight days later, October 26 dawned with appropriate drama. Full-bellied clouds pushed through the sky. *If I don't go swimming,* I thought, *I'll never make it.* I'd felt my mother's strength course into me as we clasped hands. I'd felt a peace and connection by sitting at her side while everyone else hovered or scurried. I knew that sense of calm came, in part, from doing what I had to do. And now I had to swim. She would have said "Go," but she had been sleeping for more than twelve hours, her breath rattly and shallow.

"I'm going swimming, Momma. I won't be too long. I'll swim one for you."

Her hand responded, a faint echo of its once-firm grasp. I let it go.

Midlap in the pool, freestyle, I stopped. Treading water, I looked at the clock. 11:35. I finished the lap, and did one more, backstroke. I remembered petaled rubber bathing caps with buttoned straps, I felt chlorinated water up my nose when I swam to the bottom for a painted stone, I heard my mother's laughter and the clapping of her hands. I sat on her ankle as she bobbed her foot up and down and sang, *"With rings on her fingers and bells on her toes, she shall have music where'er she goes."*

I didn't rush home, but I didn't dawdle, either. As I rounded the top of the hill where my parents' house first comes into view, I saw the familiar brown exterior, the fire escape painted neutral beige, the shuttered bedroom windows. I walked inside and climbed the stairs to the dining room. The hospice nurse sat in a chair, writing something on a pad. Bea, our favorite home-care attendant, stood next to Mom's bed.

"Did she die?" I asked.

They looked at me. "Yes," Bea said.

I dropped my gym bag and walked to the bed and asked them to leave me alone with my mother. When I saw the death certificate later, the time noted was 11:35 A.M.

AT THE MEMORIAL service for my mother, I chose to read from Paul's first letter to the Corinthians, a passage so over-quoted that it can seem cliché. But it's not the fault of the words that we've overused them. They are still beautiful and pure and revolutionary—and, as Dylan said, "easy to understand." I stood at the podium in the choir at Grace Cathedral and cleared my throat.

"If I speak in the tongues of mortals and of angels, but do not have love, I am a noisy gong or a clanging cymbal," I read, dry-eyed because I'd practiced the night before, sobbing. *"Love is patient, love is kind,"* I read, as I recalled my mother's impatience—and my own. *"Love is not envious or boastful or arrogant or rude; it is not*

irritable or resentful; . . . It bears all things, believes all things, hopes all things, endures all things." She'd been arrogant and irritable, of course, and so had I.

Yes, I'd been dutiful and responsible and had told her the truth about what she'd been afraid to ask. I'd vowed to take care of my father and Dylan—a task the details of which I could not yet imagine—and to have my own life, too. I'd sat by her side and held her hand and lifted her onto commodes and into wheelchairs. But that's not what made me her "wonderful daughter."

"I'm so lucky," my mother used to quote a friend of hers: "My children believe everything I tell them."

Mom's response, as she liked to repeat, had been, "I'm so lucky: Mine don't believe a thing I tell them."

I had learned at my mother's knee the importance of independent thinking and questioning every assumption—even her own. And yet despite our testiness and defensiveness, despite my "moodiness" and "difficulty," I'd been her "wonderful daughter." Maybe even because of it.

I read the whole passage without getting choked up, even the part about "when I was a child," thinking as I spoke those words, *my mother's child.* I raised a chuckle by pronouncing *prophesy* three different ways before moving on. I rose to the occasion.

Hours later, though—after I'd stood in an ad hoc receiving line and been held by person after person, after the blur of the reception and the lamb chops on platters passed by waiters and my cousin putting his feet up on the table at the Pacific Union Club (which made me smile, knowing how my mother would have rolled her eyes); after the surreal return home to a house without her but not yet without all her things; after I was back in my own apartment—after all that, I knew what I'd done in choosing a passage that, at the end, reads: *For now we see through a glass, darkly, but then we will see face to face.*

She was ten years old that night on a sleeping porch among the redwoods, seeing through the glass darkly. Now she saw face to face. Now she was in the mystery she'd glimpsed then and broadcast each time she talked about it.

I was alone at my desk when I realized this. The enormity of it seized me.

I'd been listening all along.

MY MOTHER HAD died in the morning, and late that afternoon, there was no longer any reason to wait.

"You wanted to show me something?" I asked Dylan. "Let's go." I grabbed our sweaters and we headed out the door. "Where are we going?"

"It's a secret."

"Where?" We leaned our bodies to climb the hill toward Divisadero Street.

"The Presidio."

"Where in the Presidio?" The Presidio is a large place, almost 1,500 acres, with lots of trees and hills and dead ends. There are several entrances, the closest to my parents' house through an old gate no longer accessible by car but regularly used by pedestrians, dog walkers, and possums. Dylan and I headed in among the eucalyptus.

"Where?" I asked again.

"I'll show you. Come *on.*"

We headed west beneath the gnarled cypresses and behind the baseball diamond and the playground and up and over some sand dunes. He stopped at the top of an ivy-tangled hill. "Close your eyes," he said. "Hold my hand."

His smooth face and wide eyes were serious but showed none of the loss he'd known in ten years. He wasn't thinking about Grandma's having just died, he was teaching me something. "It's a game we learned in camp. It's called the trust game, because you have to trust me."

"Okay." I grasped his hand.

"Don't peek."

"I won't."

I tried not to, as he led me down the hill, a step at a time.

"Okay, there's a bump here. Bend a little, there's a branch. I'll hold it out of your way. Now move to the left, just one step, okay, now stop. Now down." Like toddlers learning to walk, we took the steps both feet at a time before moving to the next. And then he stopped. "You can look now."

I opened my eyes on a nondescript plot of dried grass, circled by an empty road. I looked farther: a patch of green, a willow tree. We walked to it. I read a plaque that explained how Spanish soldiers had used this spring to water their horses. And then I walked over to where my nephew stood at the edge of the bur-bling water, dense with watercress after six months without rain.

CHAPTER SIX

A year to the day after my mother's death, I went to see a grief counselor at hospice. Mom had been showing up in my dreams. We both knew she had died but it didn't matter, it felt so good to be together again. She lived out in the country in a big white house and walked out to meet me as I approached. We had a lovely time, sitting in the sun, talking and eating. Her gleaming front teeth; her broad hands and ringed fingers; her smooth, almost hairless arms; her voice: She was vivid and so familiar that I woke suffused in warmth and unable to believe it was "only a dream."

It wasn't. As I told the counselor, whose name was Christine, I'd been with my mother. "I miss her so much," I said. "I never realized how much I depended on her. I mean, she could take over, and she sometimes drove me nuts, but she was always *there.*"

Unlike my father, who had greeted me upon my recent return from a business trip with the announcement, "We've got a crisis on our hands." Dylan had stayed home in San Francisco with Dad for three months after Mom died. With the new year, Dad and I had taken Dylan back to boarding school, where he was struggling with homesickness and grief and asking to come home. Dad was frequently overwhelmed at being a newly single parent, especially a single grandparent who had a hard time with limits and felt guilty about not being a "normal" father. "He just won't take 'No' for an answer," Dad often said, his voice ratcheting into panic.

I'd already seen my father's indulgences of Dylan. And now, in the absence of my mother, I saw how he struggled to make—and carry out—the tougher parenting calls. I watched Dylan accumulate an alarming collection of expensive belongings, including a Movado watch that "reminded him of Grandma."

"Dad!" I protested. "He's eleven!"

"Say what you want, he does have good taste. And he shouldn't be deprived."

It had often stunned me to see how vastly Dylan's sensibility—for opera, classical music, French cuffs—differed from that of his origins. It made sense, I supposed, given his New England schooling and his upbringing by grandparents made flush from my father's success as a corporate attorney. So who, I had to wonder, was really feeling deprived? When my father said, "I don't think your mother or you understands that boy like I do," his eyes got a misty, faraway look. But I didn't speculate on my father's emotional motivations then. I just retorted, "Mom would have a fit."

"Well, your mother's not here," Dad said, lighting a cigarette. "And I'm doing the best I can."

If Mom had been there, she would have dealt with this latest "crisis" by listening to Dylan and soothing his tears and telling him that he was staying just where he was. Which is just what I suggested Dad do. "You're right," he said. "I know you're right. Thank you, honey. I don't know what I'd do without you."

His gratitude and sincerity touched me, and I felt guilty for my impatience. Dad was struggling, and I knew it. But that was the other thing: In his pain, Dad sometimes gave off the implication that he alone was suffering without Mom.

"If she'd been there to greet me after a trip out of town," I told Christine, "she would have asked about me, too, and not just looked to me as a sounding board. I love my dad, but sometimes I feel invisible."

Tears sprang to my eyes. I hadn't realized how put-upon I'd felt. Dad wanted my advice, but he didn't seem to absorb any of it. "What was that you said yesterday?" he called one day to ask. "About how I should respond when Dylan says he won't go to camp?" And yet, when I suggested Dylan pick up the soda cans lying around the living room, Dad reminded me that it wasn't *my* house. Dad and Dylan and I had gone to Hawaii right after Mom died; every afternoon at five, just as I was heading out the door for an evening swim, he called to me with the exact phrase I'd heard him speak to my mother at cocktail hour: "Here's your glass of wine, honey."

Perhaps, I wrote in my journal and confided in friends, all this wouldn't have weighed on me so heavily if I hadn't been the "good girl" in the past. And if I cultivated more in my own life to balance out family duty. Grief, after all, hadn't been the only thing on my mind when I made the appointment with hospice.

"I promised my mom that I would have my own life," I told Christine, "but I haven't quite figured out how. I'd like to meet someone. You know. A man."

"She would want that," Christine said now. "She loved you." I nodded, wiping my face. *This much.*

"You know, Jesus is madly in love with you."

I looked up. Where had *that* come from?

Christine wore a silver cross around her neck; I'd noticed it when she'd met me in the waiting room, and I'd wondered why hospice had matched me up with a chaplain. No one had asked about religious affiliation when I'd called to make an appointment. Now that cross gleamed as she leaned forward, a big smile on her face. In the hour we'd been talking, I hadn't mentioned church, or prayer, or God. How'd she know I was a practicing Christian? It's not like I wore a sign on my forehead. I may have worn a cross, too—my mother's, engraved with her name and given to her at age ten—but I would've tucked it beneath my shirt.

She's reassuring me, I told myself. *She's letting me know that someone besides my mother loves me unconditionally. She's telling me that a man won't solve all my problems. She's doing her job.* I told myself these things, but the funny thing was, as I held her gaze I realized I didn't need to. Christine's sincerity let me accept what she was saying. Her eyes were steady and intelligent; she was stating the truth, as she saw it. Now I just had to find out what it meant.

I'D BEEN PRAYING for five years. But I didn't "talk to Jesus." I couldn't think of the phrase, in fact, without putting it in quotation marks. Jesus wasn't my best friend, and he certainly wasn't my lover. For that's what "madly in love" sounded like, and I'd never known that with anyone. For Jesus to harbor any kind of intimacy with me sounded like the reductive fundamentalism, along the lines of that vision I'd had in Centering Prayer of a dark-bearded man, of which I harbored such skepticism. Never mind the implication of wild, unbridled passion. I'd been in love and known how it felt to be the object of a man's desire and caring, but never "mad love." In fact, at times, I doubted I was capable of it. I'd spent eight years in celibacy, after all—during the deepest trough of my brother's addiction, I'd told my therapist that there was no more of me to give away—and recent relationships had only deepened my fear that I was incapable of love with a man. Was I slated to spend the rest of my life taking care of my family? Was being single karmic payback for all the guys I'd pushed away during my prime baby-making years?

I can be aloof, not the easiest woman to approach. "There's no doubt," an editor told me one night over drinks, when the conversation turned to a book she'd just acquired that grouped women into types like Gamine and Girl Next Door: "You're a Cool Sophisticate."

Friends were more direct. I scared men away. I was snooty, judgmental, too picky. Even Dylan, at five, had announced that I looked better when I smiled. I'd heard a lot of advice about joining an outdoor club, taking a class, going online, and—everyone seemed to agree—keeping my faith to myself. "Whatever you do," one married friend said with a shudder, "don't mention church!"

I'd scared off one fellow when I'd mentioned, in what I thought was a casual, tangential way, my involvement at All Saints'. But faith was important to me, and I didn't want to play games. In fact, if prayer had shown me anything, it was that I could be myself—which included my relationship with God.

I'd felt God's love as warm embrace, as a spoonful of syrup, as floating on the surface of water. I'd seen it in the sky outside the window, in the knowledge that my mother lived in me as surely as she had inhabited my dream, in that moment with Blake. Jesus was, to my mind, a man who'd lived two thousand years earlier as well as the son of God, a revolutionary and beloved teacher as well as the resurrected Christ. Jesus spoke in parables, Jesus resisted his listeners' desire for pat definitions. The kingdom of heaven, the Jesus I knew said, is like a mustard seed, a bride trimming her wicks, a landlord who pays even the lazy laborers for a full day's work.

I was used to this Jesus and comfortable with the definition of heaven—not as a fluffy pastel cloud with angels and pearly gates but as something that couldn't be defined. It could, however, be experienced—and that was more than enough.

One morning, writing about prayer, I reached for the dictionary. *Webster's Tenth* defines prayer as "an address to God or a god in word or thought, a set order of words used in praying, an earnest wish or request, or a slight chance" (as in "He hasn't got a prayer"). I then looked up the word in my red leather Prayer Book. Prayer, according to the Catechism, is "responding to God, by thought and by deeds, with or without words."

Both definitions rely on God being there in the first place, a huge stumbling point for many, as it had been for me. But the dictionary definition implies that God is waiting behind a door for our knock, whereas the Book of Common Prayer suggests that God has been calling to us all along.

Through prayer, I'd opened that door. But I was still checking IDs. I'd had that brief moment on the hillside in Healdsburg, when I'd felt the terror of an all-encompassing love; I'd felt fury at God for not stopping my mother's cancer. But I had not spent much time in the presence of that which made me uncomfortable.

"Jesus is madly in love with you." I couldn't get what Christine had said out of my mind. One morning I made my coffee, carried it to the armchair by the living room window. "What does it mean?" I asked out loud as I sat.

The answer came from outside the living room window, just to the left of the palm tree that grew from my neighbor's cracked cement back patio.

It means I know your name.

Warmth suffused my body, as though the sun had cleared the rooftop to the east. (It hadn't; I looked.) Tears filled my eyes. This, I knew. I'd named my baby brother, after all, and in so doing, staked my claim. And recently, a girl in the Sunday school program at All Saints' had introduced me to her Raggedy Ann.

"Her name is Madeline," Elizabeth announced, as I pulled up an extra chair for the doll.

"Nice to meet you, Madeline," I said, thinking, *She must be reading the Ludwig Bemelman books.*

"Yes," Elizabeth said. "And I named her, so I have to take care of her."

I already felt drawn to this child, looked forward every week to welcoming her to the story circle, where she'd sit next to me on the floor and rest her arm on my thigh as I modeled the cross-legged posture the children were to follow. I had recognized curiosity and eager intelligence in her eyes. But now I recognized the kind of moment that makes teaching worthwhile. The gospel of John—the story of Jesus as the good shepherd, which I had told a few weeks back, complete with laminated plastic white sheep and a sleek black wolf—tells us that "The sheep hear his voice; he calls his own sheep by name and leads them out."

Elizabeth had gotten the message. And now I did, too.

When Mary Magdalene goes alone to the tomb and finds Jesus' body gone, she sees a man she thinks is the gardener. Until he speaks her name.

"Mary," he says, and then she knows.

"Rabboni!"

She is face to face with the risen Christ, the first disciple to see Him.

I recalled the moment of annunciation between Mary the mother and Gabriel, that moment of connection in the Rilke poem that had brought me to prayer in the first place. To know someone's name means familiarity and recognition, protection and responsibility—obligation even. *Love one another as I have loved you.* It means risk and danger and loss and joy and the knowledge that you are no longer alone. It means the only life worth living.

ONE MORNING, TWO months later, I found myself lying in bed next to a man. "Thank you," I said.

Aron raised an eyebrow, a slow grin sliding across his face. "You're welcome."

Aron's hands and tongue had not left my body as I fell, layer after layer giving way beneath me, but it was his eyes that held me, his eyes that watched and wanted to know. I said, with a smile, "I wasn't talking to you."

I'd met Aron at a Presbyterian church—my mother's parish as a child, in fact, which seemed a sign. Christine had given me a few ideas for meeting a man, one of which started with the obvious (if the type of thing that had always made me cringe): Churches have singles groups. Sure, some of them smacked of fundamentalism, I discovered when I Googled "singles" and "church" and "Bay Area"—but not all. One group sounded promising. On a tastefully designed Web site, it offered "fellowship for people in their thirties and forties," listing an upcoming presentation on spiritual discernment, as well as a holiday party the following month.

I went to both. As I approached the church the evening of the discernment talk, I realized I'd left my wallet at home. The man collecting five dollars at the door waved me in, saying with a grin, "Just come to Kimberley's party next month!" At the party, his was the first face I saw when I walked in Kimberley's door. He introduced himself, suggested we step out onto the deck for some air. We talked, and I noticed Aron's hands—gorgeous, long-fingered and broad, the hands of a sculptor or a pianist. Turns out he was a cartographer who also did Web site design. Cartography fascinates me, and I asked a zillion questions. We talked about fonts. He was articulate and gracious, with intelligent eyes and closely cropped hair and a sexy, sweet smile. We talked for almost an hour. I mingled with the others there, including several friendly single men, and on my way out, said good night to Aron.

"I enjoyed talking to you," I said.

"Likewise." He smiled, turning to a short woman in bare feet and a white angora dress that made me itch just to look at it. "Lindsey lives in our neighborhood." And, to me, "This is Suzie."

I felt the familiar letdown of meeting an interesting man just to learn that he is taken. And yet he'd said "our neighborhood" as though to include her—unlike men at cocktail parties in the past who'd slipped me their business cards when their wives weren't looking. Suzie gave me a weak smile and an even weaker handshake.

"Roommates?" I asked. "Or something more?" I wasn't usually so direct, but conversation with Aron had flowed easily and I'd felt more than a hint of attraction. Plus, I'd had a few glasses of wine. And if my question put him off, well, there were plenty of other men at the party.

But he grinned. "More." Suzie moved away, and I thought, *Okay, then.* And, with a kind of relief, *I can be myself.* And when we exchanged business cards and set up a time to meet to talk about work at our local coffee shop, there was nothing sneaky about it.

The ease of our exchange at Kimberley's party stayed with us over coffee, as we spoke about the frustrations and limitations of freelancing and moved on to family and therapy—all the while steering clear of jargon as we laughed about our hang-ups and tics. Knowing he was taken, I felt an almost giddy absence of second-guessing. Since my later years in New York, and increasingly since grad school and teaching in San Francisco, I'd become more comfortable around men. *Aron could easily become a friend,* I told myself as I walked home from the coffee shop. Getting to know him would widen my circle, I reasoned, bring me to more parties like Kimberley's, where there might be available men.

A week later, he joined me as I ran errands in the neighborhood. As we stepped around some schoolkids sprawled on the steps outside the library, he mentioned wanting children. "As soon as possible."

"With Suzie?"

"No, she's not the one."

"Oh."

So he wasn't so taken. But he still lived with her, and I'd already suffered through one guy who'd lied about his status when I was twenty-six. Aron, however, seemed honest, eagerly giving me the full story on everything I asked about. In fact, about Suzie, he'd told me a few things I didn't need to know, including that she'd had a boyfriend in high school who'd committed suicide.

That night, an e-mail from Aron landed in my in-box, written at 1:42 A.M. and asking if I could meet the next day. I decided to be straightforward, the way I'd been so far with Aron. This was a new, more direct me, and I liked being around her. So the following afternoon, I met him at our usual spot, and after we'd chatted through a cup of coffee, I pulled my empty mug closer and rubbed its handle. "May I ask you a question?"

He grinned. "Sure."

I took a breath. *Here goes.* "What are you doing?"

He cocked his head, smiled.

"I feel a mutual interest between us. Curiosity. Attraction."

"Yes," he said. "There is."

"But you're with Suzie."

"You should know that Suzie and I have been on the outs for months. I've known since March that she wasn't the one."

"It's December. And you still live with her."

"Separate bedrooms."

"Too much information."

"Fair enough."

Now it was his turn to pick up my mug. Without asking, he stood and carried it to the counter, where he refilled it and asked the barista for lowfat milk.

"Thanks," I said when he brought it back. "The right kind of milk. And the perfect amount."

"I've been watching, and not just what you put in your coffee." He sat down. "Listen. This is why I wanted to see you today. I've never met a woman like you. You're incredibly appealing. When I met Suzie, I was strongly attracted to her, but the sexual intensity fizzled after a few months. What remained was a caring friendship. I thought maybe the other would return. It hasn't. I've been waiting. And now I've met you and you're everything I've dreamed of, everything I thought I'd never find. I realize there's more in store for me than forcing something that isn't there."

I blushed. Inside, desire had plummeted straight to my gut at hearing his soft Texan accent speak those words—"everything I've dreamed of"—while watching his hands wrap around his mug. With very little action on my part, those hands could be on me. My skin felt taut at the possibility. And yet.

"You know, I'm just not comfortable with this. I like you, too. I like talking to you. I find you interesting and, yes, I find you attractive." I kept my voice neutral, my phrasing flat. The content was incendiary enough; I didn't want to fan the flames. If this was meant to be, it had to happen with my wits about me. I wasn't twenty-six anymore. "But I'm not about to help you cheat on Suzie. I can't meet for coffee while being attracted to you, while knowing you're attracted to me. You have to figure out what's going on with your life, independent of me, before I spend more time with you. It's just not fair otherwise. Not to any of us."

He looked at me. I held his gaze. I thought of something I'd said that morning to my friend Leslie over the phone: "No matter what happens, this has been a good thing."

And then Aron spoke. "I'm free and clear. Last night, I broke up with Suzie to see about you." He glanced down at the veneered wooden table, pressed a crumb with his finger. An involuntary frown quickened across his brow, and when he looked up, meeting my eyes, he looked as if he might cry. "I've been wanting someone like you my entire life." He cupped my suddenly-very-small hand in his. "I'm all yours if you want me."

TWO WEEKS LATER, he was in my bed.

It had happened fast, but I welcomed fast. I grabbed it. I was making up for lost time. I was thrilled, head over heels, pinching myself, and oddly, freakishly calm. Love—not to mention love for a man I'd met at a talk on spiritual discernment, a man who wasn't put off by my desktop shrine or my thanking God in bed, a man with whom from the beginning I'd felt my *real* self rather than a partial presentation of who I thought I should be—felt deeply right.

The interest and ease with which Aron and I had first talked at the party and over coffee had opened up into long talks about our hopes and our flaws, our fears and our foibles, all of which seemed charming and intriguing and nothing we couldn't work through together. Walking home from our first real date, a few nights after he'd announced breaking up with Suzie, I'd slipped my arm through his.

"You've changed my life already," he said. "Every other woman in my life would have waited for me to hold her hand, for me to make a move, and here you do this simple gesture, so lovely and meaningful."

We smiled at each other.

"And that's not all," he continued as we turned up Ashbury Street. "I left Suzie for you. I made a proactive choice. In the past, I'd have acted like a total asshole until the woman got so fed up she dumped me."

"Huh. That's one way out. Must've made it easy."

"Exactly!" He took my hand in his then, wrapping those long fingers around mine. "I was a passive-aggressive asshole, but no more!"

Not only was Aron disarmingly up front, but his mind intrigued me. I hadn't met anyone so quick since my brother. He'd published a book of maps; I had a book of stories. He had a black belt in aikido and I did twice-weekly Iyengar yoga (even if I couldn't yet do a back bend). Aron read my stories, picking up on details no one else had ever mentioned (and a few that I hadn't noticed). When I first saw Aron's refrigerator, plastered with pictures of his parents and cousins and nephew and sister, I felt relief that I'd fallen for someone who made his family a priority. Plus, I couldn't help but notice how each photo contained a flattering shot of himself. I brushed aside the suspicion of narcissism by focusing on the fact that he was photogenic.

When an e-mail showed up in my in-box with the subject heading *Take My Hand,* I hit Reply and typed *Take My Whole Life, Too.* Corny, yes, but effective. In fact, the corniness was what meant so much to me. I'd always loved certain songs, but never told anyone. Now we sang "I Will" and "If I Fell" to each other, and he didn't mind my being off-key. And when I told him my birth date, he lit up with excitement on recognizing that I'd been born on the same day as John Lennon. And then his eyes narrowed in calculation before he grabbed my hand across the table. "Hey! The night of Kimberley's party, you were the exact age that John was the night he was shot."

"Forty."

"Not just forty. One day short of two months into your forty-first year."

"Okay, but I'm not dead."

"No, but the first part of your life is over."

It was weird, yes, but seductive, too, the way Aron found meaning everywhere, especially in those things that had to do with the two of us. And my life *had* hit one of those Before and After divisions. I was used to being tentative and cautious, reserved and analytical. By the time I met Aron, I was forty years old. I'd never known mad love. My biological clock was ringing a four-alarm fire. Aron was tall, handsome, and sexy, *and* he went to church.

But the most compelling reason for abandoning my usual reticence was that, after a lifetime of skepticism and holding back, I felt the pure rush of plunging in headfirst. I'd had years of pain and loss. Prayer had opened me up. Jesus knew my name. And as Aron said, I'd "gone out of my comfort zone," not just Googling "Christian singles" but showing up at "fellowship events" where I'd known no one. Aron, it seemed, was the payoff. God could bring not only solace and comfort but intoxicating abandon. "At this rate," Aron said, "we'll have you pregnant by Christmas." A week after breaking up with Suzie, he asked when I'd be ready to move in with him. Giddy as I felt, I'd raised an eyebrow, suggested we have a few arguments first—but I loved the attention. And I loved Aron. I didn't just fall for him; I fell for a new way of being. Just like that swimmer who'd made it twenty-five laps in the pool at the Brooklyn Y one day, this new Lindsey had been incipient in me all along.

And then there was the sex.

This wasn't "pleasure"; this was essential. I didn't have to hide my sensuality under a shroud anymore; I could revel in it—with his company. Even more amazingly (and yet another sign of all that seemed right with Aron, as though he'd flipped a switch), strangers noticed it. Walking down the street, dressed the same as I'd always dressed, I found men looking at me as though I wore a brand-new T-shirt saying *I am having fantastic sex.* I didn't worry about how I looked or smelled or tasted or sounded. I couldn't get enough of Aron's skin, his mouth, his ideas. Touch didn't bridge our separateness as much as thrum with the energy of shared sensation, commingled awareness. Sex felt like spirituality. *Was* spirituality. I'd never felt such rutty, unself-conscious lust—never known that sex, in its openness and blurring, its annihilation of ego, its immeasurable soaring pleasure, could feel like God's everlasting love.

I went with Aron on his parish retreat, and he joined me at All Saints'. At the Easter Vigil that year, as I stood in the darkened sanctuary holding Aron's hand and watching the flame pass from candle to candle, I felt stirred by the beauty of the liturgy, the expectancy of the faces flickering in candlelight, the tall man at my side. There was a baptism that night and I awaited the words that had meant so much the first time I heard them, the words that asked for an "inquiring and discerning heart." I was eager for Aron to hear these words, too, to be moved by what had so moved me.

First, though, Kenneth read the Thanksgiving Over the Water: *"We thank you, Almighty God, for the gift of water."* I'd grown up thinking of "baptism" as "christening": That was the word we used, and it had to do with giving someone a name, as a boat is christened by breaking a bottle onto its hull. When I'd asked my mother what it meant in the church, she'd said something about being part of God's family. I hadn't really thought about the water—or the naming. Until now.

Early baptisms involved whole-body immersions, as do contemporary baptisms in other denominations. Aron himself had had such a dunking as a boy. I thought of Jesus receiving his baptism, and the dove descending. I thought of people bathing in the Ganges. I thought of going under when you can't yet swim, that panic where you slap and grab at the water, where you can't breathe. And I thought of how, as a girl, I'd done underwater somersaults for hours to look up through that mesmerizing scrim between water and air, that membrane through which my body so easily slipped. Even as an adult, swimming laps for fitness, I always finished my workout with breaststroke, eyes wide open and protected by goggles, to bob above and below the meniscus of water.

"Sanctify this water, we pray you, by the power of your holy spirit," Kenneth continued, dipping the paschal candle into the font three times. And then he leaned his head toward the basin and blew, rippling the surface with his breath.

Was that how it looked, magnified a zillion-fold, when a storm raged at sea? When God blew on the formless void in Genesis? *"Over [water] the Holy Spirit moved in the beginning of creation,"* according to the sacrament we were witnessing. Was that how to recognize the movement of the Holy Spirit, by its effect on the surface of things?

"That was so cool," Aron said as we walked home around midnight. "I loved the part where Kenneth blew on the water."

The morning after Aron's and my first night together, I had gone to church. Twelfth Night: Epiphany, the showing of the light to the Gentiles. The revelation of Jesus as the son of God. That's what January 6 means on the liturgical calendar. To me, that morning, as I wept with joy, it meant I'd found Jesus' mad love in the body of a man.

DAD AND DYLAN had met Aron at the All Saints' Christmas Pageant, early enough in our relationship to throw me—not only by their being under one roof but by their standing together and talking while I rushed around serving cookies and cocoa, unable to steer and control the conversation.

"Seems like an interesting fellow," Dad said later, and repeated the name of Aron's Web site. "I'll check it out." He began referring to him as "your friend Aron." And once when I said something about Aron's being six-foot-six, my dad said, "Just like Osama bin Laden."

Dad's awkward attempts at humor often came out as barbs. He'd only met one boyfriend previously, and that was back in college, when Dad had shaken Scott's hand, looked at Scott's feet in the then-popular white leather Vans, and announced that "Betty and Lindsey won't let me wear shoes like that."

The first time I brought Aron to my dad's house, for lunch, Dad served, on Mom's china, not his usual tuna fish but artichokes stuffed with shrimp salad. I was touched—as I was when Dylan came home on spring break and we all lounged around the sitting room watching Monty Python. On the couch with Aron's arm slung over my shoulder and Dylan tapping my leg with his foot, Dad watching from his usual armchair, I felt complete in a way I never had.

Dylan had always wanted me to have a boyfriend, once giving me a tea set from Japantown made, he informed me as I untied the elaborate folded-paper presentation, for a married couple. When he was five, he stared at my stomach one day as I padded into the kitchen in my bathing suit and asked, "When are you getting pregnant?" When Aron and I took Dylan camping, I got all teary watching Aron teach Dylan how to read a GPS monitor and chop wood. As Aron and I planned a cross-country trip to bring Dylan home for the summer, I felt a chord strike deep within me, a resonant chime, a blessing on all that Aron had brought to my life.

And yes, I wanted Dad's blessing, too, his assurance that what I had found with Aron wasn't a dream but solid and sustainable. I trusted his judgment completely; my father had never lied to me. So, one night at a local bistro a few months into my relationship with Aron, I heard myself mentioning Aron's plans to move outside of the city. "I'll be spending more time there," I said. "When he's not at my place."

Dad didn't meet my eyes but gave a frown of distaste. "Why in the world would Aron want to move up to the boonies? How's he going to get any work done up there?"

"Most of his work is online, Dad. He could be anywhere. And San Rafael is hardly the boonies."

My dad gave a dismissive nod, not meeting my eyes.

"You know, Dad, Aron's never going to be a nine-to-five businessman. That's just not who I fell in love with." Why was I feeling so defensive? It must be, I reasoned, that we'd never before discussed my love life. I was still a bit shocked that I'd referenced, however obliquely, Aron's and my sleeping arrangements.

Dad gave another nod, studied the menu.

Aron's occupation, in and of itself, I knew, wasn't what gave my father pause. Dad had achieved success in corporate law, but he wasn't a snob. He admired hard work, whether manual labor or pushing papers across a polished mahogany desk. He'd grown up during the Depression and World War II, moving around Oregon as a boy while his father worked for the phone company. Later, Dad had spent his summers digging ditches for the Army Corps of Engineers and Forest Service. I'd heard my father make dismissive comments about people who "thought they were owed something"—did Dad think Aron was one of them?

Since we'd met, Aron had been talking about getting a map project off the ground. He'd spoken effusively, passionately about his idea—just as he talked about our future together. I knew the vagaries of the freelance life; I knew about creative blocks. But more and more, Aron seemed to complain about his clients and dismiss my questions about his project. I'd stayed up late with him one night, drafting a mission statement and five-point plan, but both documents stayed icons on his desktop. I'd felt the familiar lump of sorrow at undeveloped potential, just as I had that afternoon on Twin Peaks at the sight of Blake's desk. One night over burgers, I'd asked Aron how the plan was going. He'd shaken his head. "What about that potential investor you were going to talk to? That guy at church?" He'd taken a slurp of his vanilla milkshake and mimicked, "'And how do you plan on marketing your idea?'" I'd looked up, startled. I knew Aron was tired of being asked that question, but I'd never heard him sound so petty and resentful.

Now, I recalled Aron's wild predictions and claims of transformations. "I love the way you call me on my shit," he'd said one

Tuesday morning as we lay in bed until the noon whistle, leaning over to kiss my eyelid, my ear, my chin.

Aron had asked if I wanted to take a premarital class at his church, too, even though we hadn't decided to get married, let alone set a date. And when he said that we needed a new car for our cross-country drive, a Subaru "big enough for a passel of kids in the back," I'd had to wonder: How would we reconcile such a purchase with our earnings and his forty thousand dollars in credit card debt?

Was all that talk "shit"? And had Dad seen through it? As much as I trusted my father, though, I just couldn't come straight out and ask. And I felt protective of Aron. So I tried another tack, voicing a question that lately had been hovering in my mind.

"Dad," I asked, once we'd ordered from the bistro menu, "do you think Mom would have liked Aron?"

"Oh, I don't know. You know your mother. She had strong opinions."

"Meaning?"

"She would have found him a show-off."

"He *is* a show-off." One of the appealing things about Aron had been the way he admitted it. "But you know, Dad, that's all an act."

"Well, you know your mother. Your mother didn't get along well with people like that."

I caught the reference. When Blake was seventeen and moved to San Diego for a brief stint at college, my parents took him to an appliance store where a salesman offered to throw in a free bicycle if they bought a TV. "We're not here for a bicycle," my mother told the man. "If we'd wanted a bicycle, we would've asked for a bicycle."

"Buddy," my brother had added, stepping closer to the salesman, "don't waste your time. My mother doesn't get along with people like you."

"Do *you* think Aron's a show-off?" I asked my father.

"It occurs to me that he might be jealous of you."

"Of me?"

"Your writing, I mean." I had begun to publish my work in magazines, some with national circulation, including a piece about being single and another, shortly before Aron and I had met, about prayer. I'd gone public with two experiences that had once felt highly personal. And Aron had read both, photocopied them, and sent them out to his family. One day, he e-mailed me: He'd scanned the prayer piece to PDF and linked it to his Web site. *You're online!* he wrote. I was flattered but vaguely disturbed that he hadn't asked my permission. Never mind the publisher's having something to say about copyright.

Aron had praised my work ethic of rising every morning at seven to be at the desk by eight. "I have so much to learn from you," he'd said. But lately, he'd been complaining about the alarm, staying in bed, surfing the Web. So I was a morning person, I reasoned; he's a night owl. We'll figure it out. But just a few days earlier, Aron had called to me from bed to tell me that my services were needed. I was on deadline, in editing mode, and assumed he was referring to some help I'd given him the night before on a Web site. I got up, went to the bedroom door with a pencil between my teeth, to find him naked and grinning, his hand on his erection.

I didn't mention any of this to my dad. But in the weeks to come, I pondered it all.

I LAY IN bed one night, staring at the window, as Aron slept, his back to me like a hill. We'd had dinner with two friends. Over coffee, he'd interrupted me, looking pleased when I called him on it. "It was the only way I could get a word in edgewise," he said later, rolling over on his arm to go to sleep.

I loved the kind of fast, free-associative, allusive, often inter-rupting conversations that we'd had with Ben and Jeff, a high school friend of mine and his partner. Aron preferred thoughtful enunciation, contemplative pauses. Aron preferred to have me to himself, just as my mother had said about my father.

But it was more than that, I thought, as I watched the striated shadows playing off the bedroom wall and recalling other com-ments Aron had made, almost in passing.

Ben and Jeff were boring.

I didn't draw Aron out enough anymore.

Aron's sister was skittish and cold.

My father had no interest in getting to know who Aron really was.

Even Aron's new neighbor was inconsiderate of his feelings, getting up so early that she woke him up every morning.

The wind sucked the blinds against the windowsill. Had he been that critical all along and I hadn't wanted to notice?

Aron started referring to the night we met, back in December, alluding to "who you were that night." Curious, articulate, inter-ested. That's what I remembered, too, when I thought back on Kimberley's party. But I also recalled noticing every other man in the room, feeling an utter lack of investment, having nothing to lose—all of which, Aron said, had made me "so hot."

Or was that because I'd been a stranger? And because Aron had been looking for a reason to leave Suzie?

One glorious spring afternoon, Aron and I drove to Bolinas. As we headed over the hills and through the forests of west Marin, Aron asked how Dylan was doing. Aron knew the outline of the story, of course, and about Blake (whom he'd once referred to as "Bo," making me think, *That name is not yours to use*). Now, as we headed through the redwoods and Olema Valley toward the coast, I filled in the details. There were a lot. When I finished, silence filled the car. As we pulled into a parking place along the curb in Bolinas, Aron said, "You know, I just knew when you started talking that you were going to go on and on."

The next week, he e-mailed from a café downtown to ask if I was busy: *you wanna take a break?* I didn't, particularly, but I knew what he meant by "break." So I replied, *Sure, I'm never that busy*. He showed up within ten minutes and we went straight to bed. In the middle of it, the breeze rattling the blinds and the sun warm on our skin, he stopped.

"What's wrong?" I asked.

He pressed his hand to his chest. "I love you, and I lust for you, but you're just not with me right now."

"What?" I propped up on my elbows and reached for his face. "Sweetie, I'm right here."

"You're just so into it," he said.

This was a problem?

And then, "You're working so hard."

I felt too confused to cry, although my voice broke when I spoke. "I'm not *working* at all. I'm with you. We're making love. There's no one else here."

" 'Making love' turns love into an object, not a verb."

"Okay," I said. "We're fucking."

IN THE DAYS that followed, Aron assured me that what had happened that afternoon in bed was no big deal. But the more we talked about it, the more hostile and withholding he sounded, and the more troubled I felt. One night, playing with his digital camera, he got a flash of me in his favorite nightgown as I walked past to brush my teeth.

"Wow," he said, studying the picture he'd just taken. "That is sexy."

I peered over his shoulder to see a blur of silk, a flash of thigh. "And it's right here," I said, rubbing the silk against his arm and lowering my mouth to his neck. He continued staring at the screen, where my head was cut off.

When we got in bed later, he claimed a sore shoulder and rolled away from my touch. The next morning, desperate to connect, desperate to find the way back to what we'd once had, I lay next to him and provided another hand as he masturbated. "If you want to turn me on," he said, "then draw me out."

Four months into our relationship, Aron and I were bound to hit some bumps. But as the strain between us seemed more than the natural attenuation of initially giddy passion, I became alarmed at the peculiar turn of events. Once, Aron and I had shared our spirituality. Once, he'd talked of finding out "who God wants us to be for each other." Now, Aron seemed the earthly manifestation of the fickle God I read about, with a chill, in the Thirtieth Psalm: *"Then you hid your face, and I was filled with fear."*

Had I been so desperate for love that I'd overlooked what now were obviously glib references to babies and Subarus, false assurances that all was over with Suzie, ready criticisms of anyone close to him? Aron had never pretended not to have issues—"I'm a work in progress," he would say, holding my hand. And I'd been single so long, and my previous relationships had been so short-lived and unsatisfactory, that maybe Aron was right: I *didn't* know how to draw him out, how to be in his flow (whatever *that* meant). Maybe I had staked too much on hormones. Maybe I was deeply unstable and insecure. Why else was I now measuring my words and watching my actions when the whole appeal of Aron, from the beginning, had been the lack of self-censoring I'd felt around him? I became snappish and fretful, imperious and needy.

Someone you love, I heard a voice say one morning, *doesn't make you feel bad about yourself.* Christine, the day I'd met her in the hospice office, had suggested that the key question in meeting a potential partner wasn't what he thought about Jesus. Instead, Christine said, "Find out what Jesus thinks of him." In other words, as I'd understood at the time, in her office, *Find out if he's the real thing.*

I got an idea. During Lent, I'd started reading the gospel from the previous Sunday's lectionary. Every week has its three scriptural selections—Hebrew Bible, epistle, gospel—as well as an appointed psalm, but I find it easy to tune out words that have been abridged, edited, cut to fit. During Lent, I'd decided to linger in the text in the tradition of Lectio Divina, in which one reads and re-reads a brief passage of scripture. Even though Lent had ended, that's what I was doing the morning I turned to a passage in Luke in which two men are walking, on the third day after the Crucifixion, to a village called Emmaus. Jesus joins them, walking alongside, and asks what they're talking about, why they're so sad. Not recognizing him, they fill him in on recent events. As the three walk together, Jesus scolds them for not getting what scripture has prophesied, that the Messiah would have to suffer. And then, as the three arrive at Emmaus, Jesus walked ahead

> *as if he were going on. But they urged him strongly, saying, "Stay with us, because it is almost evening and the day is now nearly over." So he went in to stay with them. When he was at the table with them, he took bread, blessed and broke it, and gave it to them. Then their eyes were opened, and they recognized him; and he vanished from their sight. They said one to another, "Were not our hearts burning within us while he was talking to us on the road, while he was opening the scriptures to us?"*
>
> LUKE 24:29–32

I closed my eyes, imagined a dusty road, gutted with chariot tracks and potholes. I saw three long-haired men in scratchy coarse-woven robes and leather-tied sandals. I imagined meeting a stranger on the road and feeling compelled enough to invite him to join in a meal. And I imagined sitting down to eat, blessing the food, and then having the charismatic stranger disappear.

I would have been as dim as those men on the road. I would not have seen what was in front of me until it was gone. And then I would have recalled my burning heart, my engagement.

That's it, I thought: *Engagement!* That's what had drawn me to Aron in the first place, the level of our conversation, our ease around each other. *To sit with someone,* I thought, *to be there.* That's what Jesus calls us to do. Aron and I had talked enough. No one was at fault. Our problems were an opportunity, I told myself; we could be there for each other. Working this stuff through would deepen our love.

By now I was used to interpreting ideas that came to me in prayer as God's will, or at least as God's suggestion. If Christine's comment made any sense, it made sense only in the context of prayer. What Aron and I needed to do was sit down and pray. Together.

I jumped up, phoned Aron, left a message on his voice mail. I got a response by e-mail later that day. *appreciate the thought,* he wrote. *thanks. we'll see what happens.*

We lasted another month. A month of talking in circles, of accusations and apologies and too many aikido metaphors (on his part) and tears that turned to frosty chill (on mine). In the early weeks of our relationship, Aron had counted the minutes to our meetings, the footsteps to my apartment. Now he was too tired to make the forty-minute drive to the city. One night, I phoned him and suggested I drive up to his place.

"Right now?"

"Yes."

"You could do that."

"Do you want me to?"

There was a pause. I imagined Aron in bed, propped on his many pillows, laptop open on his thighs. Was he e-mailing, working, surfing Web porn?

"Would you spend the night?" he asked.

"I suppose so." Weren't we still a couple? "I hadn't really thought about it, Aron. I just need to see you." And then my admission of need made me stiffen with self-protection. "Don't worry. I'm not going to force myself on you."

"You know," he said, "I really prefer communicating by phone right now."

Confused and hurt, I stayed in my own bed that night, convinced it was time to break up. The first sign of real issues, and we couldn't get past them. I felt exhausted, worn thin. But when I saw Aron the following Sunday and we walked to the top of a hill and looked out over the view, he held my hand, said he wasn't ready to give up on us. I looked into the eyes of the man I'd fallen for and thought, *I do love him. All right, then. We'll figure this out.* I wasn't sure how, but with him looking at me, I wasn't ready to admit we might have made a mistake.

A FEW DAYS later, I flew back east with my father for Parents' Weekend at Dylan's school. The night before leaving, I'd written Aron an e-mail, spending an hour on five lines. I said that I was sorry for making him feel neglected and reiterated that I loved him. I edited out every instance of the slightest defensiveness, any phrasing that he might read as an attack. I changed *but* to *and.* I used "I statements." *That should tell me something,* I thought as I hit Send.

From Connecticut, I checked my voice mail four or five times a day. No messages. All weekend, I was distracted, pouty, weepy. The night I got home, I walked straight to my computer. One e-mail from him, sent the night before: *hey, L, don't want you to think I'm avoiding you. I'm just really into doing my own thing right now.* It went on from there, but I'd read enough.

When I had finished crying, I walked to the phone.

He picked right up. "Hey, Lindsey."

"I can't do this anymore, Aron."

"How are you?"

"Did you hear what I said?"

"Yes. You said you can't do this anymore. And I asked how you are."

"I'm fine."

"Okay then. As long as you're fine."

"I'm fine. Good-bye, Aron."

"Good-bye, Lindsey."

I FELT ENORMOUSLY sad and disappointed, but I knew I'd done what I had to. I had a few revisions, of course. Rephrasings, really—things I wished, as I held my phone on my lap in bed at night and dialed his number, I'd said better, or not at all. I missed him, wanted to talk to him the way we once had, wanted to share something I'd seen, wanted desperately to hear his voice.

But I always hung up before the phone rang. I thought of the peace that had come to me that morning in prayer. And the days that followed our breakup had strengthened me. We clearly weren't meant to be a couple, but we'd go on as friends, after some time apart. How could we not? We knew each other so well, we loved each other still. I'd jumped too fast, recklessly even, into a relationship, but I'd learned good things from it. Aron *had* changed my life, bringing to fruition all that had been at work for years. I thought again of what I'd told Leslie, early on: "No matter what happens, this has been a good thing."

Or so I thought.

CHAPTER SEVEN

Have mercy on me, O LORD, for I am in trouble;

PSALM 31:9

I'd kept in friendly, if casual, contact with some of the people I'd gotten to know at Aron's church, so when I got an Evite from Kimberley for a bike ride in Sonoma a few weeks after ending things with Aron, I signed up. I needed to start training for a bicycle trip in the Southwest in September, and I hadn't been to Sonoma in months. Aron wouldn't be there—he was off at a family reunion, an event we'd planned to attend together—and I wasn't worried about running into any of his friends. Come to think of it, he didn't really have any friends at church. Suzie crossed my mind, but I doubted she'd show up.

When I saw her unstrapping her bicycle from a car in the parking lot where we met, I felt a shiver. Then Kimberley waved, and a few others flashed big smiles, and I thought, *We're all grown-ups. We can handle this.*

At the third winery, Suzie parked her bicycle next to mine as we stopped to rest under some oaks. We said hello, and then she smiled. "How are your father and nephew?"

"Fine, thanks." I pushed aside the vague concern I felt, as though my family were a topic she and I had in common. In fact, she and I had only seen each other once since Kimberley's party, and that had been when I'd helped Aron pack his books. "She's having a really hard time," he had whispered to me. I'd packed a box, said nothing, and left. Now I told myself, *She's just awkward. She's just making conversation.*

It was a warm summer day, the hills golden brown but not yet tinder dry, the oaks freshly green and casting dappled shade onto last year's fallen leaves. Suzie had brought along a disposable camera, and as I turned my head toward her, she pushed the shutter.

"Did you just take my picture?" I asked.

She giggled. "Yes."

I frowned. *That's strange.* She kept her oddly benign smile fixed on me, and my concern mounted. I *would* have to say something. So when I saw her pedaling alone as we made our way to the town square for lunch, I sped up alongside. "Look," I said. "I didn't think you'd be here. It's a little uncomfortable. How about we put Aron behind us?"

Her eyes gleamed like those of a sixth-grader playing Truth or Dare. She was so young, as Aron had often noted, and not just because she was only twenty-six. "Yeah, I was really upset to see you," she admitted. "But now maybe we can be friends. Aron says—"

"Aron and I broke up."

"Oh, I know." I might as well have told her the sun was shining. "You know he's seeing someone new."

"No, I didn't know that." I sighed, thinking, *That was fast.* And then, even as I knew better, I added, "It doesn't surprise me. That would be his pattern."

"Her name's Teresa," Suzie said, "and she's just like you."

Our front tires were side by side, so all I had to do was slow down and let her pull ahead. Or as my friend Linda said later, I could have run Suzie off the road. But I have always found it hard to resist the kind of conspiratorial confidentiality that Suzie's voice held, the tone that implied she and I were in this together. And curiosity got the better of me. Just like me how? Tall? A writer? John Lennon's birthday?

But Suzie, surely, wouldn't know my birthday.

And then she explained. "She has a murdered brother and a mother dead of cancer."

IN THE DAYS and weeks that followed, I would replay that moment, the way the words hung in the air, floating on the pleasant sound of her voice, before they registered and their meaning snapped into place. I would hear again her laugh as I pedaled past her, saying, "I really don't want to hear about it" and recall how, when I got home, I threw myself on my couch and burst into tears.

I felt reduced to the two worst things that had ever happened to me. Suzie was a piece of work, no doubt about it, but Suzie was only the messenger. Not only had Aron told her the facts of my life—explainable enough as one friend filling in another on the new woman in his life, except that in this case the listening friend had been the *previous* girlfriend, the woman scorned. He had also told *me* things about Suzie: She had no friends, no core; her high school boyfriend had shot himself while on the phone with her; she felt she couldn't hold a candle to me. (That's how he'd put it, the day after telling me he'd left Suzie, and I'd wrinkled my nose. "Bullshit," I'd said. "She hates me. I would.")

How had I missed the signals? I hadn't, I reminded myself—not entirely. I'd just never fathomed that they could bespeak such stunning disregard for others. Aron, I saw now, used intimacy—his and mine; his and Suzie's—as currency, a creepy kind of emotional leverage. And I'd fallen for him. Jumped right in, in fact, right in the deep end of a pool that held no water.

That's what kept me staring at the walls and cycling up and down Highway 1 on the weekends. I still had to train for the bicycle trip in the Southwest, although I considered canceling, I felt so physically ill. And getting on a bicycle had unpleasant associations. But that would be letting him win, as one friend said. And so I trained, every weekend, riding around and around Lake Merced, up and down the valleys of the San Mateo coastline.

I wasn't ready to feel angry at myself yet, or even completely angry at Aron, so I foisted my fury on Suzie. As I rode through scenery I barely noticed, I kept seeing Suzie's grin as she'd revealed her news: that disturbing disconnect of seemingly friendly affect with insidious intent—just like Jenny Waters, who in fourth grade had gotten me to reveal, during a game of hopscotch, the name of my then-current crush only to spend the rest of recess singing out, "Lindsey loves David Kennedy!"

This went deeper than playground humiliation, of course. I didn't just want to kill the messenger, I wanted to lift her by the ankles and swing her overhead and then drop her to the pavement, smashing her face like a pumpkin. *That* got rid of her haunting grin for about ten seconds, until it rose again in my mind's eye.

Soon enough, my wrath fixed on Aron. I'd already DustBusted every square inch under and around my bed, thrown away Aron's favorite pillow, washed the bedding three times in hot water and bleach. Now I carried a wobbling stack of plates he'd given me down to the basement, near the garbage, and smashed them on the cement floor. I hung a shirt he'd left in my closet on the back of a kitchen chair and shredded it with open scissors.

I'd never felt such vivid hostility, such elaborately detailed hatred. With each explosion, either real or imagined, I waited for relief. *There,* I'd tell myself—but whatever momentary satisfaction I experienced at the shattering of plates or the ripping of fabric went *pouf* as fast as that image of pumpkin pulp had. And left me with a mess to clean up.

Pamela, the day we'd talked in her office, had defined sin as separation from God. That made sense to me now, because I felt it in my bones. I felt sinned against, and in my fantasies I returned the favor, entertaining increasingly labyrinthine narratives of revenge—could I burn his house down? No, he had innocent neighbors, but maybe I could find a way to rewire his car heater to asphyxiate him as he drove to aikido one chilly morning. I imagined strangling him. I wasn't yet ready to look with dispassion on why I'd jumped so eagerly into an empty pool; I was reeling from having hit bottom.

Some friends wondered if I should contact Aron. Maybe there'd been a simple misunderstanding? Maybe he could explain it? As one male friend said, surely Aron had his side of the story. Others (including my therapist and my priest) counseled distance. "Be careful," they said. "You're too raw." And as much as I longed for Aron to explain away all the hurt, I knew how he would manipulate the situation just as he'd once twisted my arm in aikido poses.

He'd acknowledged nothing, after all. I recalled the apologies I'd made, the silences I'd received. During a brief conversation we'd had after the breakup but before the bike ride in Sonoma, I'd mentioned that we'd both hurt each other. "Yeah," he'd said, as softly and blandly as if he were listening to another conversation, and then changed the subject to tell me he'd taken to playing the keyboard at a local club. The e-mails I'd received from him since were so insultingly glib and casual that I never responded. He referred only to my published articles—*so, sweetie, you're famous!* one e-mail began, and I replied (but never sent) *So, asshole, you've been Googling me*—and to the most superficial of common experiences.

In the pool, I slapped at the water as if pummeling Suzie and Aron, but when I finished my fifty laps, I felt little release. And more and more, I felt heavy with failure.

I knew I was supposed to forgive, but I couldn't imagine doing so. Forgiveness, Kenneth said when we spoke one afternoon in his office, is not supposed to be easy. We often dole it out too simplistically, as if flipping a switch. Reconciliation cannot happen if both parties don't acknowledge the hurt.

"*Sweetie* is not only out of touch, it's toxic," Dr. B. said. "*Asshole* is the entirely appropriate word for the situation. I'm tempted to strangle him myself."

Kenneth and Dr. B. spoke the truth, I knew, but I knew it the way I know the theory of relativity. Whenever I tried to explain it, the words never quite sound right. Neither did the words of Dame Julian, or any other prayer I tried. Looking for solace, I found only confusion. Some mornings, overtures Aron had made, small kind discrete moments, came to me—when he took my hand in his and said he would never give up on us; when he spread toothpaste on my toothbrush so I'd find it ready when I went into the bathroom; when he phoned to say he was sorry for blaming me for what had nothing to do with me. I recalled the last time I'd seen him, when he reached over to take off my glasses and say, "Look at me. You're a million miles away." Maybe I had pushed him away. Maybe I did talk too much.

Prayer didn't say. The *whoo-whoo* of the mourning doves; the moan of a foghorn; the fog itself, pushing over the cypress trees: It all bounced back an awful silence.

One morning, I felt held by a loving presence, a man with long smelly hair, as Jesus would have had. Another day I had an image of an apple tree and imagined a parable: The tree looks lovely, shady, abundant, but the fruit it gives is rotten.

You curse the fruit, yet why do you still sit there, gathering it, when you know it is bad? I imagined Jesus asking, in his loving-but-scolding tone to his dim, literal-minded listeners. Each time I thought of Suzie's grin or remembered Aron's slippery smile, his face in orgasm, I would imagine a hard, wormy apple. *I don't have to pick it up,* I'd tell myself. *I can walk away.*

But the tree had been mine, and the space beneath its branches was familiar, well worn.

I DROVE AROUND the Bay Area all summer, every weekend going to a different friend's house. "It's not your fault," they all said. But I couldn't stop picking up the apples and examining their rot. Along Ocean Beach, around Lake Merced, on the narrow shoulder of Highway 1 between Half Moon Bay and San Gregorio, I'd stop my bike in stunned disbelief. One day, I pulled into a copse of redwoods, dropped my bike, and sat, forehead pressed to my knees, as the weekend traffic zoomed by, trucks rumbling the pavement beneath me. At summer's end, I flew to Las Vegas to join the bicycle tour of the Southwest. For a week, I rode from

Bryce to Grand Canyon to Zion, an average of forty miles a day, on—if I was lucky—four hours of sleep.

And as summer slid into fall and I returned home, probably in the best physical shape of my life, the violent thoughts had attenuated, as had the minute-by-minute replaying of every scene involving Aron or Suzie. I didn't feel any closer to forgiveness, but I was no longer plotting revenge. I was waking at three or four in the morning, unable to get back to sleep. I started taking little breaks on the couch, five minutes that turned into ten and then thirty and then the rest of the day, and I found myself having to move the locker-room scale down another pound or two each time I stepped on it. Climbing the stairs to class, I felt as if leaden clamps were fixed to my ankles. The back and forth of laps, once so meditative and soothing, only mimicked life's pointlessness.

When my mother was dying, we'd stocked up on Ensure, the chocolate-flavored variety, several cans of which I now found in Dad's cupboard. Mom had tried it only once, making a face to rival any child's *blech,* rejecting the flavor as much as the reason for having to drink it in the first place. But for me, Ensure, whirred up with ice cubes and milk and a sliced banana, held a bland appeal. And the same thing that had turned off my mother now gave me a certain grim satisfaction. *You're sick,* the pink cans seemed to say as I flipped one open and poured its 250 calories of nutritional supplement into the blender. *Get in bed. You have every reason to be tired.*

This was, I knew, no longer about Aron. This was another thing entirely. Aron might have triggered the fall—but what kept me sliding down a greased chute into blackness was the fact that I had so believed in him.

Waiting five weeks for Zoloft to take effect was torture, and when those five weeks became six and seven and I felt no better, I tried Celexa, and then BuSpar, and then went back on Zoloft, higher and higher doses until I reached what Dr. B. called "the upper limits of a therapeutic range."

An M.D. prescribed Ativan, a benzodiazepine. A "bennie," in the jargon of junior-high drug education movies, of *Go Ask Alice*. It worked, softening the edges the way I imagine alcohol might for others. It let me relax. I'd lie back and feel my body absorb its chemicals, feel the muscles in my jaw and hands release, feel my brow smooth out. I took an Ativan in the morning for another thirty minutes of sleep, I took one in the middle of the day when the anxiety got so pitched I thought it would kill me, and I always took one before having to teach or show up anywhere I had to act like a functioning adult. The M.D. started ticking off the "No Refill" box and suggested I keep the vial in the freezer, just to make access that much harder, and I started counting my stash of tiny white tabs as compulsively as a prisoner ticks off days. A new bottle made me cocky with the thrill of access, and a bottle nearing depletion filled me with such panic I licked the Walgreens orange plastic for every last bit of dust.

I was hardly anyone's definition of a junkie, but in my world— a world in which I rarely drank a third glass of wine; a world in which I'd watched my brother kill himself with drugs; a world in which I'd always been a good girl—I sank to new depths. As horrible as I felt, I knew a grim satisfaction. The jig was up.

GETTING IN BED, at first, felt delicious. This was just what I'd wanted those mornings as a girl when I'd pushed my Cheerios around the cereal bowl and slumped on a kitchen stool. My mother would press her palm to my forehead, touch three fingers to the region of my neck just below my ear, where I'd hope a lump had sprung up since I'd last felt for one. And then she'd shrug. "Only you know how you feel."

She was right: I *was* faking it. And I needed to make my own decision about whether staying home from school would really spare me whatever I wanted to avoid. But her comment only compounded the dread I felt with guilt, and I was left trudging off to school only further convinced of the salvation of bed.

So I did what I'd never been able to do. *Bed,* I thought as I stood in line at Safeway and felt small hammers beat the inside of my skull; *bed,* during an excruciating coffee date with a writer a friend had set me up with; *bed,* as my cheeks ached from the effort of smiling at a party I'd made myself attend. Bed: my haven, my escape, my long-denied reward. Bed: At last. I'd rush back home as if meeting a lover to strip in the hallway and pull on my musty nightgown, lower the blinds, and crawl between the sheets. Relief, sweet and deserved.

For about two hours. And then my skin's texture started to resemble old rubber bands. I slept little and got up only to pee or whir an Ensure shake—and because I was eating so little, I got up only once a day. Unless a dog started barking or a man on a nearby rooftop started jack-hammering—and then I dragged my pillow into the bathroom, closed the door, and curled up on the tile floor, my rosary clutched in my fist. I'd stare at the creases in the pillowcase, the stray hairs and flecks of my dead skin. When I drifted off for twenty minutes, I'd wake to notice that my jaw and hands had unclenched during sleep, but as soon as I recognized the sensation of slackness, I'd tense up again.

At least I'm safe, I told myself. In bed, if I closed my eyes against the pain in my head, the car wouldn't drift off the road. I had vivid images of hacking off my hands or gobbling an entire bottle of Ativan—but if I stayed in bed, I couldn't do those things. Each of them involved getting up, so I didn't get up. Staying out of the kitchen was easy, and when I finally went in to whir an Ensure shake or rummage for a Saltine, I did so without looking at the corner of the counter where the knives sat in their wooden block.

I prayed in bed, rolling further into the sheets and saying only, "Please help, please help." The circular repetition of the rosary took me only further into the spiraling of my own negative thoughts. So I grabbed and clutched it like a lifeline—and when I lost it in the sheets or it rolled onto the floor, I put it away, as if to protect it from my failure to pray fruitfully.

Sometimes, at church, the music of the hymns made me weep. But even there, I stood with tense shoulders as I gripped the pew to keep myself from slumping or falling. I took communion and I stood at the altar rail to receive anointing for healing, but I couldn't shake the desperation. I was living in the present, all right, but a present radiating with such pain that at times I cried out with it.

I read Job and skimmed Lamentations. I sought out the most despairing of the psalms and parsed them for answers. From Psalm 22, the words that Jesus cried upon the cross: *"My God, my God, why have you forsaken me?"*

Exactly, I thought. And then, *Who am I to compare myself with that?*

I read on, hands trembling:

I am poured out like water;
All my bones are out of joint;
My heart within my breast is melting wax.

My mouth is dried out like a pot-sherd;
My tongue sticks to the roof of my mouth;
And you have laid me in the dust of the grave.

And Psalm 13:

How long, O LORD?
Will you forget me for ever? how long will you hide your face
*   from me?*

My heart leapt. How long, indeed? If the psalmist could ask these questions, could describe so accurately my symptoms, then surely, if I kept reading, the psalmist would give me the answer. I turned the page.

But I put my trust in your mercy;
My heart is joyful because of your saving help.

Huh?

I stared at the words until they blurred, became as meaningless as the marks of ink they were. Had I missed something? Was I reading an abridged version? I thumbed to the beginning again, and jumped to the end. I looked up the psalm in my New English Bible and my King James paperback from college. No footnotes. No ellipses. No explanation. Just *trust* and *mercy,* those insufficient words, leaping across a gap I could not imagine bridging. I felt baited, tricked. I kept the page ribboned but stopped reading beyond the psalm's early verses.

I didn't want God anymore. I wanted only to be delivered. When Kenneth told me, one morning on the phone, that it would be a good thing for me to get out of bed, I mumbled, "Uh-huh," and hung up, thinking, *I don't care.*

AND THEN, ONE morning, the candle went out.

I had been using a short pillar for months, its wick increasingly drowning in its own wax. *That's me,* I thought, and chipped away at the hard accumulation of wax with a knife to pry out more wick. I tilted the candle at an angle to touch the flame to it, which caused streaks of black up the side of the yellow wax. The wick had become part of the solidified wax so that in chipping away at wax, I mangled wick. But that morning, the floor hard beneath my legs, the room unbearably still and quiet, I managed to get it lighted. The flame got shorter and smaller, more and more tentative, a blue nub, and then a dot. *Blue,* I thought, *is the hottest part of a flame.* It was all I had, a tiny wavering speck over a pool of wax.

And then, out.

Candles had blown out before during prayer, and I'd either let them go or reach for the matches. No big deal. But during my depression, every little thing—the growl of a dog on the street, the honk of an impatient driver, the title on a book spine as I walked past my shelves—was a big deal. *A sign, it's a sign,* I told myself.

I'm doomed.

An extinguished candle seemed not the natural reaction of a too-short wick and a quicksand of melted wax but a message from God. No there there. Not in me, not in God. And the fact that I had poked and prodded that flimsy little wick? I'd probably hastened its demise, I thought, or—worse—prolonged its life span beyond what was intended and natural. If it was ready to burn out on its own, who was I to interfere with that?

Once I'd testified about the power of prayer in national magazines, once I'd written about how it held me and opened up quiet corners. Now I couldn't even use a candle, the most elemental of props. I was a failure and a fraud.

"Open my lips, O Lord, and my mouth shall proclaim your praise," I whispered.

Oh yeah? Fat lot of good that'll do you.

"All shall be well, all shall be well, and all manner of thing shall be well."

Ha! Dream on! And then, a cackle of laughter.

I thought of Linda Blair, when Blake and I had howled at *The Exorcist* on TV to see her head creaking clockwise and her mouth spewing projectile vomit. Silly, ridiculous, lame. But the idea of possession held a dreadful power, like a scab I couldn't stop picking. The more I told myself not to think of it, the more it lured me. Like the knives in my kitchen, it radiated a seductive pull.

Falling asleep had never been my problem—it was waking up too early that besieged me. But now I feared closing my eyes on the dark. Now I feared what might rise unbidden against the backs of my eyelids: contorted human body parts and faces, like illustrations from Dante's *Inferno;* the lidless ruby red eyes from the uncut version of *Rosemary's Baby* that I had watched at age thirteen. I dreamed, one night, of finding myself in an S&M dungeon.

Did some other force, some demon, the devil himself, hold me in its grip?

A store in my neighborhood sold pentagrams and vials of gnarled roots, animal skulls, dark velvet cloths festooned with gems. Dylan had asked to go into it once when he was seven; I'd obliged but squirmed when he approached the counter and asked the salesperson, clad in Goth black, about the items. I didn't believe in a little red guy with a pitchfork and horns, but I did know that evil walked the same streets that I did, and not exclusively in a store. But I avoided its corner, crossing the street or going an extra block out of my way, as though black magic might lure me in like a dirty old man with an offer of candy.

I talked to Kenneth about all this. He listened.

"God is so huge," he said, "that God contains all things, light and dark."

"Evil?"

"God is not evil, but God knows about terror and fear and anxiety. God is good, but God is not always nice. Look at the book of Job, the garden of Gethsemane. Saint John of the Cross writes of the dark night of the soul."

Okay, I thought. *Fair enough. But what about those images, those faces?*

"It is not unusual, or a sign of evil, for frightening images to come up in prayer," he continued, as though reading my mind. "God is in prayer, and God pushes us to face what terrifies us through prayer."

This made sense, but I still felt abandoned. Once, light and succor had held me. Now they'd vanished. What kind of gift was that? I knew from reading the psalms that the gnashing of teeth and the clutches of the evildoer played as big a role as the green pastures and the still waters. But that didn't mean I wanted to spend time there.

Or did I?

Even as I struggled, something about depression had a compelling inevitability. It wasn't lost on me that I was finally doing what, on the day my mother died, my friend Leslie had said I would have to do. Fall apart. God's love had allowed me to let a man into my heart who had broken it, true, but what made me crawl—and stay—in bed went far beyond Aron. I'd pulled myself along my whole life. If I let myself feel as bad as I possibly could, the logic went, I'd be plucked intact from my despair, delivered whole from my fear. I'd force someone to save me.

I'm scared. God, I'm scared.

I wrote it over and over in my journal, in small neat print that looks foreign to me now. Each letter careful, almost childlike, as though a terrible fragility might make them—and me—burst, shattered, if I pressed too hard. Some days, though, I stabbed the page with my pen, once injuring a tendon in my thumb. In Dr. B.'s office, I felt too childlike and broken to sit upright on the couch, and lying down made me think of Woody Allen movies, so I took to sitting on the floor. One morning, in his office, I slapped my own face.

I thought of suicide, but I did not want to die. The thought of giving up made me incredibly sad, one of the few thoughts that could make me cry. I could not do that to my father and nephew. Instead, my favorite fantasy involved hospitalization. I stared longingly at the small, discreet ads in *The New Yorker* for McLean Pavilion and imagined a quiet, clean room with an open window letting in a sweet breeze. I'd climb in a freshly made bed and sink back onto pillows. Wearing a soft cotton hospital gown that was someone else's responsibility to launder, I'd read magazines and watch *Oprah*. Never mind that I never did either activity in my own apartment. The fantasy was idealized depression, the sanitized version of a breakdown. Friends would visit and confer in low, concerned voices, huddling in the doorway with attending professionals.

"Eat," my therapist said one afternoon on the phone, when I told him I'd been in bed all day. "You need to eat."

"I don't want to." My voice pleaded. *Please don't make me.*

"It's important you eat," he repeated.

"And what if I don't?"

"If you can't take care of yourself, we'll have to hospitalize you."

His straightforward tone and the word itself—it's one thing to think about it, another to hear a mental health professional speak it as the probable outcome of your own behavior—shocked me.

"My God," I said, as a tear ran slowly down the side of my face.

"OH, HONEY," Dad said.

He'd just called to ask how I was doing, and I'd told him. I usually said "about the same," as though that small hedge might let in some hope for both of us.

"I'm sorry. Listen," he continued, clearing his throat to give his best attorney-making-a-case voice. "I was thinking. Why don't you come over here and stay for a while? You can bring your computer if you want. I can do the shopping and cooking. We'll make up the couch in the sitting room. You shouldn't be alone."

I grabbed at my father's invitation like the lifeline it was. At his house, I lay on my mother's daybed and read—or pretended to, picking up a book when he walked into the room to ask how I was feeling.

"A little better, I think."

He'd pat my foot, propped up on cushions. "Good," he'd say and give a small but encouraging smile, as though he wasn't sure whether to believe it, either. If I was under his roof, he could watch over me. Around him, I didn't have to pretend. I could soak up the fact that he was taking care of me.

Dylan, too, seemed to intuit what I needed. One day, when he was home on break, I sat in Dad's kitchen staring at the glass-topped table. I was aware of Dylan's movements but too tele-scoped in pain to take them in. And then he put a plate in front of me with a bowl of soup he'd heated up and a piece of toast. "Here," he said. "You don't have to make yourself anything. I just did."

Sometimes, at Dad's or home in my own apartment, I could read. Ian McEwan's *Atonement; Jane Eyre;* Gina Berriault's sto-ries; Caroline Knapp's *Drinking: A Love Story.* I couldn't get up, but I could reach for a pen to scrawl exclamation marks in the margins of Knapp's book, where her descriptions of addiction described what I was experiencing. Ativan and bed were my bottle. I told lies ("Fine, I'm fine" or "I just ate a big sandwich"). I bargained ("Tomorrow I'll get out of bed. If I let myself have one more day in bed, I'll be able to get up tomorrow"). I rolled in shame. I licked dust from empty prescription bottles.

I pulled the Rumer Godden children's books from the shelves in my parents' sitting room, books I had loved as a girl, and reread them. Dad and I talked over dinner about these books, and what he was reading. We talked about Andrew Solomon's *Noonday Demon,* a book I had picked up with alternate flashes of fascination, hope, and terror, avoiding the chapter on suicide for months.

My father and I had always been close, temperamentally aligned, two bookworms next to Blake and Mom, who were more social and gregarious. I'd always felt a kind of emotional permission around Dad, unlike the mandate from my mother to cheer up or go do something. Around Dad, it was okay to be mopey or sad; he didn't take it personally. And now, during my depression, we spoke with an openness and urgency that we'd never shared before.

"You know," he told me one night as we finished yet another chicken-breast-and-sautéed-zucchini dinner he'd made, "I wonder if my passivity as a parent contributed to your being depressed now."

I was stunned. Dad, the quintessential straitlaced WASP, had never been one to indulge, as he put it, in navel-gazing. And yet, in the aftermath of my mother's death, he'd amazed me by going to see a therapist. He talked openly about his feelings of grief, and his abiding guilt over being what he termed "the classic enabler" with Blake. He told me about his struggles in the early 1970s, when he'd left the law firm where he'd worked for twelve years to go out on his own. "The pressure was enormous," he said. I'd always recognized my father's difficulty standing up to Blake and Dylan. But, other than the resentment I often felt, I'd never examined its impact on me.

Growing up, Blake and I had known that "No" meant "No" the first three or four times, and then Dad would give in, exasperated: "Oh, all right!" Unlike Blake and Dylan, I had never wanted to push him. Mom's brook-no-guff stance and clear limits had kept me secure. And yet I'd seen her cede to him, not because she was a pushover—far from it—but because she needed to keep him on an even keel. "You and your brother will have your own lives," she told me one day, "but I have your father to worry about." Her logic seemed an excuse, and a troubling one: Weren't we the children? Shouldn't we come first?

And yet I knew that my competent, authoritative daddy—at six-foot-two and 220 pounds, an imposing figure with a deep, sonorous voice—had another side. During the week, he strode off in crisp wingtips in the morning, the picture of an upstanding attorney, and when he came home, Blake and I knew to lower our voices. "You two run upstairs," Mom would say, smoothing down her skirt as she sat across from Dad at cocktail hour. "Your father needs to unwind."

During the weekend, Dad puttered around the garden and kitchen in his scuffed slippers, asking me to join him in a task that inevitably involved standing next to him in silent companionability as I held screws in my palm for a small repair job or pulled back branches while he trimmed a hedge. When I wanted a hot dog for lunch, he made me a hot dog, no matter what everyone else was eating; and when I changed my mind and asked for grilled cheese, he'd toss out the boiling water with the Oscar Mayer wiener in it, and plug in the electric frying pan.

But sometimes, Dad's long tether snapped. And then he not only shouted (often, it seemed, out of proportion to the incident, as on the Christmas morning Blake and I, in our excitement, spilled orange juice on Blake's new train set) but acted in odd, unpredictable ways. Several years in a row, he'd stood up from Christmas dinner at my grandfather's and announced that he was walking home. "I just can't take this anymore!" "This" consisted of my aunt's bourbon-lubricated potshots at cigarette smoking, my nineteen-year-old cousin's indictments of corporate America, my uncle's defense of Richard Nixon. Next thing I remember, Mom had herded Blake and me into the station wagon and was trailing Dad along the suburban streets, repeating, "Be reasonable, Jim," until he climbed in the way back and spent the whole drive home, an hour on the freeway, with his knees up to his chin, muttering about my mother's intolerable family. And when we got home and there was a package at the front door, wrapped in garish metallic paper, no one said a word as Dad tossed it right in the trash. I knew, although I cannot remember being told, that those packages had come from my father's brother, an uncle I'd never met. During my childhood, Dad had never said one word about his brother (he'd barely even spoken to his mother on her visits from Oregon), but Mom later told me that my uncle had come home from World War II "so spooked" by the sounds of the waves against his Navy ship that he'd lived in a hospital ever since.

Passivity, Dad had said. Was that it? I looked at his face. The expression on it was thoughtful, placid.

"Dad, what really happened with your brother? It was such a mystery to me growing up, such a taboo." I'd never mentioned this—too worried such an admission might be heard as criticism—but in the wake of Dad's comment, doing so felt natural, even welcome. "Was it PTSD, you know, shell shock?"

Dad pushed back his plate. "I suppose that played a part. In those days, they didn't understand mental illness as well as they do now. A man I used to work with suffered horribly from manic depression and couldn't function without lithium. There was such a stigma to it, but it saved his life." Dad named the man, a colleague and close friend, and I felt admiration for what my father had achieved in the business world, where the slightest hint of his own emotional frailty would have been professional suicide. Yet he and this man had had enough mutual empathy and respect, it seemed, to confide in each other.

"We live in a much kinder era now, in that respect. Thank goodness," Dad continued. "But in 1955, there were fewer options. My brother was put away."

"With what diagnosis?"

"Paranoid schizophrenia."

I'd assumed as much, but still, the confirmation chilled me: my uncle, psychotic. And then I recalled a night when I was twenty-seven years old, when I first saw what my mother meant when she said she had my father to worry about.

It was Thanksgiving weekend, and I was visiting Atlanta. My parents were living there, Dad's job as in-house counsel for a food company having morphed into deputy general counsel for a corporation on the brink of a huge buyout. Mom and Dad and I were in my father's car, going close to 70 mph, when my father suddenly lifted his hands off the wheel.

"Where am I?" His voice warbled in a tone I'd never heard from his mouth, high-pitched, panicking.

My mother reached for the steering wheel as Dad's hands fluttered above it. "I don't know where I am! Where do I go?" His hands returned to the wheel, rubbing palms against hard plastic as though to scratch a ferocious itch.

"You're on the freeway, Jim. We're driving home. We've just had dinner and we're on our way home. Everything's fine." My mother spoke calmly. "Just go straight." In the dark car, I could just see her profile in the reflection of the few headlights around us. The speedometer needle dropped steadily. I looked through the back window and watched the headlights of the nearest car: Two hundred feet away? One hundred?

"I need to get out! I need to get out of the car! I have to get out!"

Keeping my head turned, I said, "Move the car over one lane. Just one. To the right." I looked forward. "There's an exit, Dad." Then to the side again. "Okay. Good, keep going. Another lane. Don't stop, Dad. You're almost there. To the right! Good." Sweat trickled down my side.

"That's right," my mother said. "Listen to Lindsey." She pointed to a cluster of neon: Hardee's, Exxon, Dunkin' Donuts. "Here it is."

The car had slowed to 25 mph. She and I talked him onto the exit. He pulled into Exxon and threw the car into park and got out, leaving the car door open. I called: "You okay, Dad? Do you need help?"

He thrust his hand backward, a gesture I was used to from walking in the room when he was on the phone or calculating a measure from atop a ladder. *Sh! Don't bother me now!* Tears burned my eyes.

Dad walked toward the twenty-four-hour store, rummaging in his pocket for a cigarette. The car-door-open bell was binging and the car lights were still on.

"I'm sorry you had to see that, Lindsey," my mother said, her voice as steady as it had been all along.

"What happened?"

"You've never seen it that bad, have you. The first time I saw it happen, I was very nervous. I always tried to keep it from happening in front of you children. . . . It hasn't happened in a long time."

"But what is it? What's wrong? Why'd it happen now? We were just driving along."

"It's the stress about Blake, it's very hard on your father." Blake, as far as we knew, was living on the street in San Francisco. "And he's under enormous pressure at work. Your father's never been good under pressure."

"Yeah, but . . . Is he going to be all right?"

"He'll come right back as though nothing happened. He'll be fine. He always is."

Until the next time. I stopped myself. I could barely think it, let alone say it. "But—"

"I know, honey."

My mother had been right that night in Atlanta. My father did come back, stamping out the cigarette, and settled himself in the driver's seat. I offered to drive, but he said no as calmly as if I'd asked the time.

And I'd never seen him act that way again.

I pushed away my plate. How much did that episode and the factors underlying it have to do with Dad's brother? Or with my own depression?

"You know," I said in a conversational tone, "I read somewhere that paranoid schizophrenia often kicks in in the late teens or early twenties. When did you know your brother was ill?"

"That sounds about right. Early twenties."

"So you weren't aware of anything growing up?"

He shook his head. "No. Oh, he chased me with a hatchet once, but that's just regular kid stuff."

"My god! Dad!" I stared at him. "That is *not* regular kid stuff."

"Children can be very cruel."

That night, I could have asked more: when, where, how, why. The pure acceptance and freedom I felt in this newfound verbal intimacy with my dad—prompted, perhaps, by our talks about grief, about Aron, about my illness—had opened a door into my despair, brought a sweet breeze through to stir up the cobwebs and dust. That night, as we continued sitting at the table, neither of us getting up to clear the dishes or turn on a light as the sky outside the window grew darker and finally black, the enormity of what my father had told me seemed enough.

A few days later, I turned to him in the kitchen.

"Daddy, am I going to get better?"

He was standing at the counter, going through the mail. "Yes, honey, you are. I sure hope you are."

"Look at me. Please look at me."

He looked at me, took off his glasses. My father's eyes were blue, "as blue as the waters of Lake Louise," he used to quote his fifth-grade teacher as saying, and now I saw them as if for the first time. All my life, my dad had worn glasses: horn-rimmed, tortoise, or gray plastic, white and worn where he chewed on the arms' edges as he read the paper or leaned back in his chair after dinner. But, now, without his glasses between us, I noticed the bed of soft wrinkles around his eyes, the soft lines of skin.

"Yes," he said. He put his hand on mine. "You have your mother's strength. You are going to get better."

Tears filled my eyes. His words were those of a father's love for his child, yes, and as such they carried familiar comfort. But they held something new, too—a seriousness of intent and meaning. We had deepened the bedrock of trust and compassion between us—not just as father and daughter, but as adults. I knew I wasn't over the hump, but in the months to come, I would remember his words, pulling me back from a place far, far away. And I would believe him.

I HAD STOPPED writing. My class had ended. Freelance work had dried up in the aftermath of the dot-com bust, and I tried to find more jobs but didn't have it in me. I was barely making rent, denting further into my savings. My parents had always been supportive of my decision, at thirty-two, to start working as a freelance writer and teacher. Dad, in particular, seemed to honor the choice I'd made, probably because he (unlike Mom, who'd been taken care of financially by men her whole life) knew what it meant to earn an income. When I'd finished my novel, in Virginia the previous year, I'd called to tell him. All choked up, he'd told me how proud he was.

Now my father offered to help me out financially. I felt like a failure accepting his offer, although he made it in a loving and unencumbered, if characteristically blunt, way: "Look," he said as I stared at the floor, "it's going to be yours someday anyway."

I had a class coming up; could I cancel it? Yes, I could. I phoned my department head and said I had a family emergency and had to go back east. "That's the truth," a friend said. "You are your family." I flew to New York, where Michael found me a sublet for a month. One single-digit-temperature night in Greenwich Village, as I walked up Sixth Avenue after a dinner party, I felt a vitality I hadn't known in months. Wearing a blue velvet dress and fleece-lined boots, on streets lumped with recent, still-white snow and glittering with neon and traffic and streetlights, I felt both anonymous and wholly myself, my face tingling from the cold. *This is what I need,* I thought, as if New York City were a person, a glitzy and noisy but loyal and dear friend.

I spent lots of hours curled up in the sublet, as the steam heat banged and hissed. I saw friends and walked in Central Park and visited my former therapist. I saw many movies and started several books—*Seabiscuit, Win One for Jeeves, Mrs. Dalloway*—as though a new genre might hold my interest. But each I put away after three or four pages. I couldn't write, but I took my laptop to the New York Public Library, where I sat in the Rose Reading Room and read my novel aloud to myself in a whisper.

Dylan visited on weekends from boarding school, an hour's train ride away, and I took him to *The Lion King* and the City Ballet and Blockbuster, where we rented Monty Python and Japanese anime. I joined the West Side Y, and when friends asked if I'd been to the pool, I'd tell them yes, which was true.

"Good," they said. But I'd think, *It's not good at all. It did nothing.* My body felt so fragile and rigid as I trudged up the steps to the pool, my bathing suit bagging on my flattened hips. And when I got in the water, I winced at the contact. After fifteen or twenty laps, I got out, feeling no different. I didn't float.

I went, one Friday night, to the Whitney with a musician I'd met at a party. After the museum, we walked through the dark park to the West Side, where we had dinner. As we talked about the morality of standing among other hip New Yorkers to *ooh* and *aah* at the quilts made from old mattress ticking and denim overalls by Alabama sharecroppers, I picked at my salad. John suddenly reached across the table for my hand. "Are you okay?"

My hand felt stiff and small in his warm grasp.

"You're so on edge," he said, his eyes kind.

I nodded, biting my lip to keep the tears from spilling. "I've been having a hard time. Anxiety. You know." I shrugged in an effort to deflect his concern. "But I'm okay. You're sweet to ask."

The next afternoon I phoned him. He picked up and I burst into tears. "I'm not okay at all."

"Oh," he said. "Uh. Can we talk later? I'm on my way out the door to a recital."

"I'm sorry. Never mind. I'm okay." I hung up, mortified. I barely knew John, and I'd acted so alarmingly, so inappropriately. And yet, in a way, I felt some relief. At least I'd done something.

I wanted, that weekend, to die. But I felt so heavy with lethargy, so bleak with apathy, I barely had the energy or will to open a can, let alone kill myself. I did, however, have a homework assignment. I'd signed up for a workshop at the Writer's Voice at the West Side Y in the hope of kick-starting a proposal I needed to finish. Homework was always a strong point: Give me an obligation, and I'll fulfill it. But that weekend, turning on the computer to write a one-page synopsis of my book idea felt both monumental and pointless, utterly impossible. I crouched on the bed for a good forty minutes before being able to get up. I managed to open the Word file (I'd already written a synopsis, a year or two earlier, and all I had to do was print it), looking sideways at the screen while flinching as though being forced to watch a torture scene.

But I printed the page. By Sunday night, I could call John and apologize. Dr. P., my New York therapist, called, and I talked to her from the kitchen while I boiled water for pasta and made a sauce. And the next day, when I phoned Dr. B., I could tell him that I'd gotten through. The way, I suppose, a weekend of drug or alcohol bingeing is gotten through: in a haze that feels timeless, a constant present as the sky lightens and darkens outside the window until you emerge, Monday morning, blinking, to find yourself on the other side.

ON MY WAY to the West Side Y that month, I would pass a homeless man who sat against a plywood barrier at a construction site at Broadway and Sixty-third. He never looked up or said a word to me; the cardboard sign propped against his crossed knees grew bleary and streaked from snow and rain and a brief warm spell. And then, one day, he wasn't there.

I felt a guilty relief, and then, the following morning, while clutching my rosary in bed, instant recrimination: I'd never given him my coat.

That's what Jesus tells me to do, after all.

If entering the kingdom of heaven were easy, Jesus wouldn't have been a revolutionary. If I called myself a Christian, I needed to do a lot more than go to church and say a rosary. If I followed the path of Jesus, went through that eye of the needle, stayed on that narrow path, I needed to do the uncomfortable, the risky, the downright terrifying. I had to love my neighbor in action as well as words. And I had failed. Not only hadn't I given the man my poufy and warm coat when I could have easily gotten another— or even brought him a cup of soup—but I hadn't even looked him in the eye. I'd never even noticed his face.

I felt a horrible shame.

The feeling was familiar.

I had no reason to be tired, and if I did, it was because I'd made the moral flaw of feeling sorry for myself. My mother had never said that, of course, nor would she have. But in my child-hood conflation of her messages, I'd absorbed the wrong lesson. Just as I'd accepted feeling responsible for Blake, and later, for Dylan, I'd believed Aron's accusations that I hadn't drawn him out enough, although I'd known that wasn't my job. I'd wanted a partner so much that I'd looked the other way on the warning signs. Why, I'd put up more hurdles for God than I had for Aron!

The image of the homeless man's huddled form returned to me. *To see Christ in our fellow human.* I couldn't place the source of the phrase, but I heard it crystal clear. Another task on that narrow path, another task I'd failed. I hadn't even been able to pray for the guy—I'd sat down with every intention of doing so and turned prayer into a self-pity party.

This is not *compassion,* I told myself that February morning. *This is* not *the kingdom of heaven.*

And why should I trust the kingdom of heaven, anyway? The last time I had, I'd plummeted to the depths. Prayer had sent me Aron, after all; prayer had made me lose my inhibitions. And what had prayer done for me since? I felt heartbroken, frustrated, deeply disappointed, petulant. So much for trying it the right way, the devoted way, the gentle and polite way. So much for being a good girl.

I blew out the candle, clutched at empty air.

CHAPTER EIGHT

Darkness is not dark to you, O LORD,
the night is as bright as the day.

PSALM 139: 11

One Sunday morning back in San Francisco, an associate rector at All Saints' told a story. A man is in his house when it starts to rain. The rain doesn't stop, becomes a flood. Waters rise. A neighbor knocks on the man's door. "We're leaving. Come with us!"

"No, thanks," the man says. "God will save me."

The rain keeps on. The water reaches the windows, trickles over the sills, pours into the rooms. The man climbs to the second story, from which he sees more neighbors rowing a boat toward his house. He waves them on. "Thanks anyway! God will save me!"

The rains continue. The house is almost entirely underwater by now, the only dry spot a patch of roof where the man sits. A helicopter hovers overhead, a rope ladder drops within reach, and still the man won't leave.

"I'm waiting," he shouts over the roar of the engine and blades. "I'm waiting for God to save me."

I RETURNED TO California, my father meeting me at the baggage claim and searching my face as I walked up to him, as though looking for an outward sign that a month in New York City had done the trick. And then he looked away toward the carousel, as it started lurching and honking into motion. I'd made the mistake of letting him pay my medical bills—it was either that or more debt—and when I gave him Dr. B.'s statement for the month I'd been away (a month of phone sessions), Dad took it without a word. Later he called me to say, "I hate to do this. I'm not complaining about the money. But there are three sessions a week here! I thought you were getting better!"

Dad was understandably concerned that my depression had gone on so long—nine months by the time I returned from New York. Yet his reaction to Dr. B.'s bill made me feel that I needed to justify the frequency of my sessions, and their content—and that angered and hurt me.

That morning I'd blown out the candle in New York, something in me had snapped. I didn't want to go through the motions anymore, not when the motions—those of my mind, masquerading as prayer, and those of my resentment around my family—felt so wrong. Attributing depression to self-absorption and pride seems cruel, if not inaccurate. But, looking back, I recall the heady petulance of what felt like a long-overdue temper tantrum. Justified, yes, but so narrowly viewed through the prism of my own pain that I couldn't see yet anything beyond it, not even God.

When Dad and Dylan and I were together, in our reliable if not always easy triangle of seventy-two-year-old man, forty-one-year-old woman, and adolescent, I felt caught. I went on trips to Parents' Day at Dylan's school because I wanted to see Dylan, and because my dad asked me along. Simple enough. But then, at lunch with the other parents, or even picking up a rental car, I found myself injecting "Dad" into every sentence so as not to be confused for Dylan's mother and my father's trophy wife. During teacher conferences, as Dad settled into a hearty camaraderie about the weather and air travel, I frowned and asked about academic performance. At restaurants, I shook my head when the waiter offered Dylan another Shirley Temple. I felt increasingly compelled—by my anxiety and, yes, by my father's passivity—to act the Enforcer to his Rewarder. After all, when Dylan wanted a Palm Pilot to "organize his notes," he waited for me to leave the room so he could explain to Grandpa why he wanted to go to the mall.

I no longer felt as comfortable spending my days at Dad's house—the novelty of my depression had worn off, and I needed to get back to my own place, to try something more than lying in bed, however powerful its pull remained. I felt increasingly impatient hearing about Dylan. Mom had been gone for almost three years; how long was Dad going to keep complaining about rearing Dylan "all alone"? When Dad sat across from me at dinner and recounted Dylan's latest scheme to cover his bedroom walls in rice paper, I rolled my eyes as Dad marveled, "I've never seen a child with such persistence"—or "creativity" or "imagination." *What about me?* I'd think. *What about Blake?* And then I'd feel pathetic, a grown woman jealous of the attention being bestowed on a thirteen-year-old.

Except in those moments, I wasn't grown. I was eight years old, listening through the bathroom wall as Blake squirmed out of a consequence. I'd stopped formal prayer because I was fed up with being the good girl in front of God; I certainly didn't want to keep up the façade in my family.

So what would take its place?

SPRING MOVED INTO summer. One foggy night, I walked into Langley Porter, the psychiatric facility of UCSF, a soundtrack swelling in my mind. I just didn't know what tune it played. While in New York, I'd been assigned an article on grief, and I had phoned Langley Porter for names of people to interview. I'd taken down a few names, and then I'd heard myself ask the switchboard operator about depression groups.

"We have two types," she said. "Partial hospitalization and CBT."

I had a friend who had done a CBT—Cognitive Behavioral Therapy—group. Wearing my professional hat, as though it were all for research, I asked for more information. When the operator said the first step was making an appointment, I wrote the term *intake evaluation* with the same thrill I'd felt when I first read *benzodiazepine* in my Ativan literature.

Several weeks later, I sat in a small windowless room, filling out a questionnaire. "I think of suicide. . . . I like people. . . . ❏ Never ❏ Occasionally ❏ Frequently ❏ Daily." I was given a fat white three-ring binder with a clear sleeve over its cover; under the sleeve, a pale blue sheet read, in large boldface letters, "MAN-UAL FOR GROUP COGNITIVE BEHAVIORAL THERAPY OF MAJOR DEPRES-SION: A REALITY MANAGEMENT APPROACH." For the next twelve weeks, I carried that binder on the street and on the bus and kept it by my bed so that, every night, I could fill out the mood chart, numbered 1 (WORST MOOD) to 9 (BEST MOOD). But first, I took out the pale blue cover sheet and put it back in, blank side out. I grimaced at the line drawings accompanying the text: spiraling arrows (Rumination); cartoon faces labeled STUPID and UGLY across their foreheads (Unhelpful Thought Patterns); wiggles radiating from stick figures (Blame).

But I clung to my binder. My intellect was insulted, but I wasn't worried about my intellect. So even as I rolled my eyes at "Step One: Consider that doing pleasant activities is important," I found myself repeating the phrase as I forced myself, one week, to get up and walk through Buena Vista Park every morning. I didn't feel any better, but I could tell myself I'd gotten up. I could say I'd done a pleasant activity. And I liked the word *Consider:* It didn't promise easy, instant recovery. It didn't make any promises. It knew what we were up against.

IN JULY, DAD and Dylan flew to London, and I joined them there a week later. When I arrived at the hotel room, I found my father unable to meet my eyes.

"This is it," he said, turning away from me as soon as he opened the door.

"Hi," I said, but he kept talking. "They'll bring up a cot for you later. It'll fit between the sofa and TV." He didn't move but stood just inside the doorway, jiggling the change in his pocket. I peered around him: a sofa, two chairs, a desk, and two twin beds pushed together beyond which an open door gave a glimpse of the bathroom. With a cot set up, I wondered, how would anyone walk around the room? What if I had to use the bathroom in the middle of the night?

"It's kind of tight, isn't it?"

"I wanted to see what you thought."

"Let me put my bags down." He still didn't move or look at me. "Excuse me, Dad." Annoyed now, and worried, I pushed past him. "I could get another room."

"I thought of that," he said, standing by the window now, "but I don't know how you'll find one. They're full here. I asked."

"This is London. There are lots of hotels."

He shook his head and heaved a sigh, as though I were being unreasonable. "I don't know where . . ."

The desperate edge in his voice, combined with my jet-lagged bleariness, steeled me further. At one time, sharing a hotel room with my father and thirteen-year-old nephew might not have bothered me, especially in a city like London where, presumably, we'd be out and about during our waking hours. Since Mom's death, the three of us had traveled—and stayed in hotels— together comfortably, even happily. But I usually had my own room, or at least a bed around the corner from theirs. Sleeping on the cot felt reminiscent of crowded one-star hotel rooms when I was a backpacking college student—a jolly enough situation when you're twenty years old and traveling with friends but decidedly less appealing in a room scattered with Dylan's dirty socks and electronic devices.

I walked to the desk and sat in the chair, pulling open the drawer for a phone book. I looked up "Hotels" and found a listing across the street. I phoned. They had a room.

My father watched me place the call as though I'd been speaking Urdu. When I hung up, I stood and announced that I was going to get settled, take a short nap.

"Stay awhile. You just got here. We'll have lunch."

"None for me, thanks. I'll just grab some peanuts from the minibar. I need to sleep and take a shower. Then I'll be fine and we can walk around, have an early dinner."

"I've found the best way to get over jet lag is to stay up as long as you can, all day the first day. Get right into the new time zone. That's your best bet."

"Well, that's not what I'm going to do. I need a nap."

I was bleary, exhausted. But most of all, I wanted to flee my father.

He sensed it, erupting into a shout: "Oh for Christ's sake!" And then his voice cracked upward in pitch, so that he was almost screeching. "Stay! Don't go! Please don't go!"

I sat down.

"I haven't talked to an adult in a week! I'm going out of my mind!" Standing next to the desk, my father was ruffling the pages of a guidebook over and over, his fingers so agitated I thought he might rip the book into confetti. "I'm at my wits' end. I'm at the end of my rope." He took off his glasses and rubbed his eyes. "It's not his fault, it's all my fault. I've indulged him. I've spoiled him. And now I'm losing control. He gets these ideas and there's no stopping him."

"What ideas? Where is he?"

My father swatted the air with his hand. "Oh, every day it's something new! It never ends! He's gone off to a sword shop in Camden Town. He went there on the Tube. He studied the route on the map, only had to transfer twice. He's such a clever boy he'll be okay. If not, it'll all be my fault, of course. He'll get there and find out it's not Knightsbridge and come right back."

"Sword shop?"

"Don't criticize me! Please don't criticize me!" His voice climbed again. What I was seeing made a certain sense, the dark underbelly of those dinner-table confidences he and I had shared, the latest plot on a graph that had started somewhere in his child-hood, maybe with a hatchet, and continued through those drives home from my grandfather's house and that night in Atlanta. And yet, as his daughter, the only other adult in the family, I was terri-fied. With an almost clinical detachment, as though studying a dis-play, I watched as he let go of the book to rub his hands together.

"Dad, you've got to get a grip. You're the adult and—"

"Don't yell at me! Please, whatever you do, don't yell at me!"

I stood up, walked into the bathroom, shut the door, turned on the fan, sat on the toilet, put my head in my hands, and tried to breathe. When I emerged, Dad had pulled himself together so that when Dylan walked in, Dad ruffled his hair and said, "Have a good outing, honey?"

That night, I dressed for dinner in a blue silk dress I'd had for eight years and a pair of nice, if worn, high-heeled shoes. As I crossed the street to Dad and Dylan's hotel, I promised myself I'd do all I could to promote what Dad would have termed a "pleas-ant evening." I was the other adult, after all; I should act the part.

As soon as Dylan opened the door to their room, however, I felt myself bristle. He was dressed in a suit; that didn't surprise me. What made me feel like Cinderella was the tie around Dylan's neck. I'd seen it earlier, in a store window. Not just any store, but Hermès, on New Bond Street; when Dylan and I had passed earlier, he'd stopped and pointed. "Do you like that tie?"

"It's okay," I said. "I don't much like pastel ties. And it's for a businessman in his forties or fifties. Totally inappropriate for a thirteen-year-old."

"Why are you always so negative?"

So now I knew where Dylan and Dad had gone earlier, while I unpacked. And as much as I could justify my disapproval (indeed, dismay) at the purchase, I felt haunted by Dylan's criticism. More and more, with the two of them, I *was* negative—the naysayer, the party pooper, the pill. I'd become someone I didn't much like, and I couldn't see my way out.

Seeing the expression on my face, my father rolled his eyes and whispered to me, "It came out of his allowance."

I replied full voice. "Then he gets way too much allowance."

"Shh!" my father hissed, waving his hand as though flitting away a bug.

"What's your problem?" Dylan asked me, his eyes stubborn and steely.

"*The* problem is that you have an unhealthy sense of entitlement."

"*I* don't have a problem."

None of this, of course, was Dylan's fault. But I couldn't help myself. I felt like a child, too. So I spoke like one: "You will if you keep getting everything you want."

"Oh, stop it!" My father's voice rose, authoritative now, deep with protest. "Just stop stop stop stop it, Lindsey!"

"Oh, I see. It's my fault. I'm the bad guy." I turned around. "You can't keep doing this, Dad. You can't lean on me time and again and then treat me like the harpy. I've pretty much had it."

"Oh, for Christ's sake," my father said. "No one treats you like the harpy."

My mouth tasted pennies, my ears rang as they had back in 1976 at my first rock concert. Part of me was nine years old, mortified at having stirred up my father's wrath. And part of me was indignant, blinded by fury and frustration. As ashamed as I would later feel, I couldn't see my way then to any other role; I'd been in this one for what felt like forever.

"Harpy!" Dylan barked a mirthless laugh. "What's a harpy?"

"A hard-ass," I said. "A bitch."

"Stop! That's enough, I said!" My father trembled from head to toe. "Let's go. Let's go, for once in our lives, and try to have a civilized evening."

We left the hotel and walked down the narrow sidewalk to the taxi stand. Dylan reached for my father's hand and, unable to see another choice, I followed.

THE FAMILY SITUATION got better after London. It couldn't have gotten much worse. I realized how much resentment I'd been bottling up, and how I'd walled myself off from my dad's desperation. I started to extricate myself from my self-appointed, self-justified role of acting *in loco parentis* to my father. *Authority,* I reminded myself and the friends to whom I confided, was the key word. I had none. I felt plenty of responsibility, just as I had with Blake, but I had no power, no control. And my dad *was* at his wits' end, but he was my dad. He had been there for me; I wasn't going to walk out on him. Besides, I understood as I never had when my father couldn't stand up to Dylan or, before him, Blake: Dad was afraid—deeply, irrationally, utterly—of confrontation.

One morning, still in London, my father and I sat on a

bench in Hyde Park, as Dylan rode a horse around the park with a hired guide.

"We've got to work together," Dad said, "not at cross purposes. You've got to let me be the parent."

Chastened, I apologized. And then I explained how difficult it was to stand by when I disagreed with Dad's decisions. Plus, I said, "Sometimes, Dad, you lean on me too much."

My father admitted his feelings of being lost and overwhelmed at not being able to control a willful boy. We conferred on what could be done to, as Dad put it, "ease the situation."

I backed off. After all, I'd seen a side of myself I didn't much like. I'd relied so long on feeling trapped that I'd begun to see no other venue. Whose "fault" was that? I saw more clearly my own defensiveness, my readiness to blame others when I felt caught. I'd become so used to feeling put-upon that I hadn't always acknowledged my role in getting myself there.

HEALING, WHEN IT came, did not make the neat trajectory of an upward climb to match the plummeting fall. It held no such emotional imperative, no such narrative thrust. It happened in fits and starts. The crowning moment did not come on schedule. I had written *Healing* on the front cover of a journal I started in July 2002, three weeks after that Sonoma bike ride. While I must have felt some glimmers of recovery (otherwise why would I have written it? Even wishful thinking has to have some basis), I would have to cross a long, dry desert before I was better—in my mind and in the relieved faces of those family and friends who showed me I'd made it out. During those fourteen months, though, even in the most challenging times with my father, the most despondent troughs of despair, there were moments of oasis.

I briefly dated a man who made me laugh and couldn't keep his hands off me. Kissing again was bliss. Discovering that my body hadn't forgotten how to respond didn't just restore my sense of sexuality; it restored some sense of self.

I took a tutoring job for several weeks, helping a high school sophomore with her English essays. I always took an Ativan before driving up the hill to Elizabeth's house—a drive that, once, I would have walked—not because tutoring was so horrible but because the moments leading up to it were. By the time I was sitting on the leather couch, Elizabeth's knee pressed into mine as she sat cross-legged next to me with her iMac in her lap, the tension in my arms, neck, and jaw had softened.

One Monday, we worked on her conclusion for a paper on *The Great Gatsby*. She paged through her worn and highlighted paperback for a passage she wanted to quote.

"Here." She opened the book between us, her long strawberry blonde hair falling forward like a curtain.

"Read it," I said.

[H]e must have felt he had lost the old warm world, paid a high price for living too long with a single dream. He must have looked up at an unfamiliar sky through frightening leaves and shivered as he found what a grotesque thing a rose is and how raw the sunlight was upon the scarcely created grass.

I pulled the page closer, scanned the words that had me holding my breath.

My God.

There it was: everything that made me love to read as a child, that made me want to write. There in front of me was not only the gorgeousness of Fitzgerald's prose but the precision of the most accurate description of despair I had ever seen. Unfamiliar sky. Frightening leaves. Raw sunlight and tender, fragile, scarcely created (*scarcely!* What a choice, for the ephemeral quality of creation!) grass.

I had read those words at least ten times before in my life, but never like that. As Elizabeth tapped away, I couldn't wait to get home, where shelves of books awaited me. That day, I couldn't wait to write.

A FEW MONTHS later, at the Christmas concert at Grace Cathedral, I listened to the sweet purity of boys' voices, including that of Dylan next to me. I'd been in bed all day, rousing myself half an hour before Dad was due to pick me up. I got in the shower and then crawled back into bed, wrapped in a towel. I managed to get dressed and drank a cup of coffee as if it were just a normal morning rather than six P.M. At the concert, during the singing of what the program identified only as a traditional Scottish carol, the boys' bell-like voices asked, *"Where is he, where is this babe?"*

Listening, I felt the tug of hope that I had experienced on finding anguish articulated in the Thirteenth Psalm, despair described in Fitzgerald's novel. Someone else had put into words what I'd been feeling. Just where *is* he, that Christ child, that salvation for the broken world?

The boys' voices rang out the answer: *"Right in front of you, the* LORD *our Savior."*

Advent is about waiting, and Christmas is the payoff. As perplexing and as beautiful as that seemingly abridged psalm I'd given up on: He is right here. The kingdom of heaven, Jesus says, is all around you.

I thought of the day Dylan had made me a bowl of soup and piece of toast. I thought of what my father had done for me, and my friends. I thought of that awful day in London, and the fact that here we were still, side by side. Relationship. Incarnation. Salvation. Wasn't that the message of my faith? Wasn't that what had eluded me? I'd been searching so hard for something that had been in front of me the whole time.

My hands trembled.

Christmas morning, I woke early, as I had as a child when Blake or I crawled into the other's bed so neither had to be up first. Alone now, I sat by my bedroom window from six to seven-thirty and watched the faintest hint of daylight turn into full morning.

ONE FRIDAY, I flew to L.A. to see Michael, who was staying at his parents' house. As with any change of scenery, I fixed on the possibility of instant recovery. Once in Michael's parents' guest room, however, my small duffel unpacked, I lay on the bed and crawled under the covers. It was four o'clock in the afternoon. Hearing Michael approach, I grabbed a book in the pretense of reading.

"Chop chop," he said from the doorway, snapping his fingers. "Time to walk the dog. Come on. Up. You're coming. *Up,* Lindsey."

We walked the hills of Laurel Canyon and ran errands and deadheaded lavender and babysat his niece and nephew. At the end of my second day there, he drove us to Santa Monica. I started crying on Mulholland Drive, as we waited for the light to change before turning left down into the valley. Michael held my hand, spoke my name. I let myself absorb that. He drove past UCLA and the verdant wealth of Westwood and then, at the coast, he pulled into an empty parking lot. We changed into our suits behind towels and open car doors. Except for a couple lying near the empty lifeguard chair, we were the only people on the sand as we walked toward the water. The sun was low but not yet set; the Pacific gleamed gunmetal before us.

"Oh my God, Lindsey." Michael had stopped, grabbed my arm. "Look!"

Not twenty feet away, just past the break, five dorsal fins sliced the surface of the water. Michael and I stood as the pod of dolphins breached their way south, their bodies sleek and dark, all arching graceful muscle.

I felt it first on my lips. They parted, and then it spread, moving up my cheeks to touch my eyes and soften there, then down along my jaw and neck and arms, until my whole body relaxed. A smile, my first natural one in months. Tension slid away, warmth flowed inside and around me. I laughed, ran for the water, dove into a wave.

"My God," Michael said. "You're renewed."

God might as well have sent a shaft of light on me. Come to think of it, God probably did—the sun was setting over the Pacific, after all. But what made that moment—and the forty minutes that followed, as we swam and bodysurfed—full of divine grace was not so much God's discreet hand reaching down from the clouds as my feeling held in the interconnectedness of all Creation.

I'd been christened as an infant with drops from the baptismal font at St. Stephen's, but I'd never felt reborn until I ran
into the water and threw my body into that curling wave. I was
no longer Lindsey in pain, or Lindsey at all, but part of a magnifi-
cent, beautiful whole. *I am in trouble,* depression says. *Help me.
How can the world go on?*

But the world does go on, and the world was created good.
Amazingly, mysteriously good.

And when I came up on the other side, the wave now broken
in foam on the sand, I had seen the hand of God.

I HAD WANTED God to save me from my flooded house, just as I'd
once wanted my mother to give me permission to stay in bed. But
by waiting for God on my own terms, I'd missed God on God's
terms. In CBT, no one asked what had "caused" my depression—
not that no one cared, but that the reasons didn't matter as much
as the small steps I began to take. And as weeks of 1s and 2s on my
mood chart began to climb—in short-lived peaks of 5s and 6s
before plateauing back to 3s and 4s—I saw that deliverance
wasn't going to come. My mother wasn't going to let me stay in
bed. She was dead. Even God, I had to meet halfway.

That was the leap of the Thirteenth Psalm, that bit the
psalmist didn't explain. He didn't need to. The answer had
already been given. *"Right in front of you."* The rhetorical turn in
the psalm, the response of the Scottish carol, my moment in the
Pacific: They come at the place where petition turns to praise,
where we stop asking and start seeing. *"Heal me, O LORD, and I
shall be healed,"* says Jeremiah 17:14. *"Save me, and I shall be saved."*
I thought of the morning in New York, a week before I'd flown

home, the morning after the biggest blizzard in six years, when snow buffeted the city and blurred the straight edges and lay, thick and white, across the gray branches outside the window. I'd given up on formal prayer, but even in depression, I hadn't been totally blind. "It's beautiful," I'd said. "Thank you."

One Sunday morning, the gospel reading came from Luke. Jesus has cleansed ten lepers, but only one, a Samaritan, has stuck around to thank God. Jesus asks where the other nine went. *"Were not ten made clean?"* (Luke 17:17). The implication, as with most of Jesus' questions, is clear. The other nine have scurried back to daily life.

Later that day, as I drove down Masonic Avenue, a voice came out of the radio. *"Wise men say, only fools rush in . . . "* NPR was playing a recording of Elvis, but it wasn't Elvis I heard against my hair, lips brushing my neck, breath hot in my ear. *"Like a river flows surely to the sea, darling so it goes, some things are meant to be."*

As the car came to a stop, I smiled.

When Kenneth had told me that forgiving Aron right away might be not only impossible but dishonest, I'd asked what I could do instead. "I don't want that hate," I said. "I don't want to carry it forever."

"Pray for him," Kenneth said. "Ask God to forgive him, ask God to stop the pain from going any further."

That seemed too mild for someone I had wanted to strangle. *Listen, God! Listen to what happened to me!* I wanted to shout from the rooftops.

Kenneth continued: "God knows what happened." He paused, pursed his lips in consideration. "Find one of the angriest psalms. That might help."

I searched my red leather Prayer Book for where the enemies perish and foes are crushed. *"Let them,"* I read from Psalm 63, *"be food for jackals."*

What sweet permission! Not only could I say some not-very-nice things, but I could quote them directly from the Prayer Book! Anger was okay with God, after all. What solace, too: I didn't have to be nicey-nice. Prayer, in fact, demanded that I not be. That's why, I realized, my lip had always curled when I'd tried to pray for Aron. Doing so felt false. God didn't just know that; God understood it.

On a hike one day, a friend told me about *metta,* the Buddhist cultivation of lovingkindness, in which we ask for well-being. For ourselves, for those we love, for those we don't even know, for those we would like to feed to wild animals. "Everyone," Eve emphasized as we hiked among the trees of Muir Woods. Later, I tried it: "May Aron be healthy and safe. May Aron be happy and strong. May Aron know love and peace. May Aron be safe from inner and outer harm. May Aron be at ease."

For a while, my lip continued to curl at the shape of his name. So I stopped. But slowly, I began to feel a softening. An odd, unexpected kind of softening—more detachment than tenderness. I saw him as a being wholly separate from me, as if I'd never known him. Some days I couldn't speak those words whose emotions I wasn't ready to wish on him—happiness, say, or love—so I stopped at those I could. Gradually, I found I could say his name without snarling. I understood how a man who feels unloved by his parents might put down others as a way of feeling better. I prayed that the cycle of hurt would stop.

One morning in prayer, an image of Aron sitting on a hillside came to me. I hadn't been thinking of him, and there he was. "I forgive you," he said.

What? *You* forgive *me?*

But the warmth did not diminish and I felt, just as palpably as I'd once felt his hostility, that he'd let go of me. At the end of our time together, I'd felt his judgment directed at me, the woman of his dreams whom he'd fallen for one night at a party and then watched turn into a flawed, imperfect human being who didn't draw him out enough. Narcissism, plain and simple.

For him, okay—but that was only half the equation. I'd wanted desperately to love and be loved; I'd willingly suspended all disbelief; I'd been so angry I'd wanted to kill him, and Suzie, and then I'd turned on myself. Now, God was showing me that Aron didn't blame me anymore—and I didn't need to, either.

I saw why forgiveness had been so difficult. I had severed the last link.

It had taken seventeen months, but I had come to see that what I had felt as God's love had been, indeed, God's love. God had made it available—the way, I thought, God gives us free will. It's up to us what we do with it. I'd fallen in love, and the fact that the man I'd fallen for turned out to be someone else wasn't God's fault, or mine. What mattered wasn't clutching my rotten apple but understanding why I had picked it up.

That Sunday in the car, I thought how I would have been one of the nine lepers, checking healing off my list. *Okay, all healed now; next?* But Elvis's voice on the radio had reminded me to stop and thank God. Mad love hadn't lasted, but it had held me for a time. I had known that which terrified me. The best parts, the parts I'd once thought Aron had unlocked, were still mine. Had been, all along.

I left it at that, and drove on.

AIR, IT TURNS out, is not empty. Our hands move right through it, as mine had that morning I'd blown out the candle. But like the Pacific I floated on in Santa Monica, air carries molecule and association, memory and particle, a compound as rich as any stew.

Time, I found, had conflated. When a friend referred to the two years she had been out of the country, I was thrown; hadn't it been only one? When asked my age, I said "Forty," and then, "No, wait, forty-one. I think." Well into the new year, I was still writing the previous year on checks. I couldn't recall months on end. Gray hair and crows' feet didn't show until I was feeling better. Delayed reaction, I wondered, or delayed perception? And did it matter?

That February morning in New York City, when I'd blown out the candle, I'd given up on formal prayer. But prayer, it seemed, had not given up on me. God's hand had been there to take me out of my pain all along; I just hadn't been ready to reach for it. When I marked a 5 on my mood chart, I wept with gratitude. A few weeks later, I reached a few 7s, and even an 8, and then I knew I'd pulled through. It felt the way that those twenty-five laps in the pool at the Brooklyn Y had felt—exhilarating, yes, but reassuring and oh so familiar. *This is the way it's supposed to be. I'm back.*

CHAPTER NINE

You will change them, and they shall be changed.

PSALM 102

Every May for the past three years, I have gone to Tassajara, the Zen Buddhist Mountain Center in the Santa Lucia Mountains of California, east of Big Sur. In a narrow valley that slices between six-thousand-foot-high peaks covered in madrone and oak and laurel, Tassajara Creek rushes cold and loud, especially in May after record-breaking rains. I go to take the waters—stripping down to nothing and easing my body into rock- and tile-lined "plunges" of up to 110-degree mineral water fed by hot springs. And when I get good and hot, I walk down the smooth wide rocks into the creek itself, so cold with runoff that I yelp as it laps against my bare feet. Crouching, I splash my chest and face. *All of me,* my skin cries. *All of me.* Especially that region of my back, between and below the shoulder blades, that the splashing can't reach. I take a breath and dunk, whole body, arching my neck to get my head all the way under.

For the three or four days I'm there, I can't avoid the sound of the creek. Not that I'd want to. The sound of splashing and falling and trickling and gurgling and roaring is constant: in the cabins where the residents and guests sleep; in the zendo; in the dining hall; in the bathhouse. Most of the time the sound recedes into background, like birdcalls or a breeze on my skin. And then it startles me, catches me off guard, with the surprise that it's been there all along.

During contemplative prayer—the rosary, say, or Centering Prayer—I've had the sensation of a current running through me, like that creek. In my nose and out my mouth, it's alive, elemental. My face, in fact my whole body, seems a mask through which it flows. The words slip away, like the beads in my fingers and the edge of the pool when I float—a container for what happens within. I lose sense of time, of physical location. And then my toe bumps the edge of the pool or my finger hits the bumpy bead at the end of the circle, and I'm back. Back to the world. Back to my day.

O Lord, we float on your breath. O God, we ride on your love.

COMING BACK TO a regular prayer routine, I wandered a bit aimlessly between the rosary, the psalms, the Daily Devotions. Each felt familiar, reassuring—if not always transcendent. That was okay; I knew not to expect instant liftoff every time I closed my eyes. But I felt a bit restless as I moved around the apartment, looking for the right spot, the most natural posture. And then I'd recall running into the ocean, diving into that wave, and remind myself that any approach could work. Sometimes, we don't learn what's right until after the fact.

One March morning, my father and Dylan and I drove up to the top of Mount Tamalpais. When my mother had died, we'd known what to do: cremation, followed by scattering the ashes "somewhere beautiful," as she had put it. But finding the actual spot had taken three and a half years. Immediately after her death, we'd talked about the Russian River, Sonoma, Stinson Beach, even Hawaii. To each option, my father would say, "We could do that." But I wanted her ashes someplace we could easily visit, the way I walked on Ocean Beach because we'd scattered Blake's ashes off its shore. Dylan wanted Grandma's ashes in an urn, the more elaborate the better. But Mom wasn't the ashes-in-an-urn type, and—as I'd reminded Dad—she'd been claustrophobic. "Remember how spooked she was that time she got stuck in the elevator at Gump's? I don't think we should keep them in the box."

"She's not really in there," my father told me, as though I'd missed a key point.

But when I'd picked up the box with Mom's cremains, as the mortician called them, a few weeks after her death, I'd placed it—rigid maroon plastic, sharp-cornered, surprisingly heavy—on the passenger seat of my car and started laughing, tears running down my cheeks, as I strapped it in with the seat belt and locked the door. "How does this thing work again?" she'd asked every time she got in or out of my car.

I'd taken that maroon box to my apartment and I'd opened it. There was the tag I'd spotted on her toe when "the ghouls," as Dad referred to them, came to get her body. Now it was fastened to a twist-tie around a plastic bag, a kind of liner to the box. I untwisted the tie and looked in the bag. There were pieces of bone, creamy white against the ash. I took a pinch, rubbing it between my fingers and then rubbing my fingers into my neck, my scalp. I scooped a small amount into a Limoges box and later

I took some up to Sonoma, where I sprinkled them over a field of California poppies.

We chose a plain green "granite" box in which to keep the ashes until we decided what to do. We dug a hole in my parents' front garden, in a spot with lots of afternoon sun, and placed the box like a stepping stone. Dad planted two white azaleas. I tried not to think about that elevator at Gump's. And when my dad told me he talked to her every morning when he went out to get the paper and I found myself glancing over at the green box every time I walked in the gate and climbing up to dust its surface and palm its warmth when the sun was on it, I felt a kind of resigned peace. It wasn't perfect, but it would do.

And then my dad sold the house.

"We always said this was temporary," he said, as he leaned on the shovel and I bent my knees to reach in for the bottom of the box and lift it out. And then, a couple weeks after Dad moved into a new apartment for himself and Dylan, I noticed the box on a bottom bookshelf, next to an old Yahtzee game and a carousel of poker chips. I picked it up, dusting it with my palm, and carried it into the living room, where my father sat reading the *New York Times Book Review*.

"Dad."

My father frequently didn't look up when I walked into the room. Now he tapped the open newspaper with his finger. "You know, I tried reading that *Da Vinci Code* book . . ."

"Dad." I held the box in front of me like a tray with a drink on it.

"Oh," he said. "I know." He sighed.

"We have to do something," I said, sitting down next to him. "I have an idea." I'd never forgotten a spot I'd visited in college, on the western flank of Mt. Tamalpais, near the summit of the "over the top" road, as we called it. Oak trees, I told my dad, and an unobstructed view to the Pacific and, if you looked south, the city. I described the beauty, the quiet. "I think I can find it," I told him.

But we agreed, as we headed up Mount Tam that day in March, that it didn't have to be the same exact spot. Each turn of the car around a bend offered up undulating green hills, banks of California poppy and lupine and sticky monkey flower, the ocean where a squiggle of darker blue marked the tide pushing in. Any spot would do.

We parked at a pullout where there were no other cars. The ridge isn't particularly high or steep, but as we crested it, a breeze ran up the mountain from the ocean. We stepped into it and made our way down the rocky narrow trail. We were surrounded by rolling slopes of grasses and wildflowers that ran, uninterrupted, down to the ocean. The sky was clear blue, the view of Stinson Beach and the lagoon and, beyond it, Bolinas. Straight ahead sat the jagged Farallones. A woodpecker worked in a pine tree, and a turkey vulture soared over a copse of oak trees. The quiet felt like that in a cathedral when the people and music go away, but even more so.

Looking for a spot we could easily find again, we stopped near two lichen-covered rocks. I knelt and untied the plastic bag. I looked up at my dad, who gave a small nod, and at Dylan, who watched. I held the opening of the bag close to the earth, the way I pour potting soil into a planter. I spread the ash with both hands and combed it through the long grass. Two screws, gray with dust, fell out. I picked them up.

"Will you look at that," my dad said.

"What is it?" Dylan asked.

"Grandma had two hip replacements," Dad said. "Sometimes

she set off metal detectors in airports." And then, patting Dylan's shoulders at the appearance of some fond, private memory, "She hated making a fuss."

I placed the screws on one of the rocks. (As of this writing, they're still there.) When the plastic bag was empty, I turned it inside-out and rubbed it against the grass. We placed pink ranunculus on the blanket of ash. I stood up, careful not to dust my hands on anything that wasn't skin or grass or earth. My father stepped toward me, and I moved slightly as though to let him pass. But he stopped, gathered me, and then Dylan, into his arms.

LEAVING MY MOTHER'S ashes on Mount Tam seemed to release all of us. Dylan became increasingly independent now that he was in his fourth year of boarding school and no longer crawling into bed with Dad the way he had for months—"to see if I'm still breathing," as Dad put it. Despite repeated pleas to come back to San Francisco for ninth grade, Dylan announced that he wanted to stay another year at his boarding school and start high school in tenth grade.

"I'm so relieved," my father said, choking up on the phone when he called to tell me. "God, I'm relieved. He made the right decision." And then, sounding wistful and a bit amazed, "He's growing up."

Dad, after forty years of two to three packs a day, quit smoking. He'd contracted bronchitis, as he had every winter—but that year, it didn't go away. In fact, after a weekend at Lake Tahoe, where he struggled to climb the steps of our rented condo (and smoked on the deck), it turned into pleurisy. And then into congestive heart failure.

I arrived at the hospital just as Dad was admitted into a room. The oxygen had perked him up. I stood holding his hand, and when the ER doctor came in, Dad spoke before the doctor could: "I'm no fool. I know a wake-up call when I see it. You don't have to give me a lecture. Just get me the patch."

He asked me to throw away all the cigarettes in the house, from the freezer—he stored cartons for freshness after buying them at Costco—and from his dresser. "Go through every drawer," he told me. "And don't throw them in the trash. I'm likely to go down there in the middle of the night and dig them out. Take them off the premises."

Always skilled at cooking, Dad now talked about blood pressure and salt intake with the same relish he'd once shown smearing beef Wellington with pâté. He'd amazed me by going to a therapist; now he joined a gym. He seemed more resilient, less anxious. But he still complained about having too much time alone. When I suggested he join a group or call his friends for dinner, he had a ready reason why not. "Those groups are full of geezers," he'd say, and "No one wants to be around a lonely old man."

Through our long talks, our moments of tension and confrontation, our mutual reliance over the past few years, I'd come to understand my father better than ever. And yet he was still— even more so—the daddy I'd felt so comfortable around growing up. So, when he began to act in ways I'd never seen, I didn't know what to do.

Six months after leaving Mom's ashes on Mount Tam, Dad returned from a trip back east visiting Dylan. He complained of jet lag, of hotel food, of the cattle-car experience of modern travel. All that was familiar. But when he'd been home for a week, and then two, and was still mentioning how weak he felt, I wondered aloud if he should go to the doctor.

"Oh, it won't do any good. He'll just make me take a bunch of tests. I'll get better. I just need to get my strength back."

He agonized over Dylan's high school applications, planning the agenda for completion months before their due dates. "I think I've finally got it under control," he said every day in October.

What could he be doing? One Sunday, during our weekly visit, I asked.

"You have no idea," he said. "You've never seen applications like these."

"Dad," I said, and smiled, to soften what might seem like criticism, "I've done a lot of applications. I'm on the market for a teaching job, remember?" But maybe Dad didn't want to remember that; after all, I'd interviewed for positions in the Midwest and South. None had panned out, but I knew he'd considered the potential ramifications if I'd been given an offer. "I'm good with forms," I continued. "You had a secretary for forty years. Let me help."

He stood in the doorway, wringing his hands. "I hate to impose on you."

"Believe me, Dad, I'd rather do it myself than see you get so stressed out."

"Well, thank you, honey." Immediately more perky, he headed off to the kitchen. As he put dinner together, I went through a tall stack of manila envelopes, my eyes widening and my dread climbing as I found photocopy after photocopy, duplicates, originals, some filled out partially, others cut and pasted with strips held down by tape. There was no rhyme or reason, just a pile of checklists and busywork. I took the files home and got to work.

Every day, he asked, "Are they done yet? Don't forget the test results. Has Dylan written the personal statement yet?" And every day, I told him not to worry, that I had it under control. "Trust me," I said.

"It's not that I don't trust you . . . ," he'd respond, wringing his hands, and then not finish the sentence.

I was used to my father's anxiety and complaints, and to his always bouncing back. Now he stopped working out, saying he was too tired. He missed a lunch date with out-of-town friends. One afternoon, he tripped on the kitchen rug and fell. He burped at the dinner table and hung his head, picking at his food. And he expressed, more and more, a desperation and meanness that, even in his wildest moments, I'd never seen.

I begged him to call the doctor.

"I'm going tomorrow," he said one Sunday, as I parceled out his weekly meds. "Happy now?"

Feeling sneaky, I called the doctor first thing the next morning to voice my concerns. Dad, I knew, would brush aside all the recent episodes, not even mention the fall. The receptionist put me on hold and then came back to say no, Dad wasn't scheduled for ten o'clock. In fact, he wasn't in the appointment book at all.

"Tell you what," she said. "I'll call him and say that you phoned just to see if he made it in okay"—I had offered to drive him, because I didn't want him to get behind the wheel, and he'd promised to take a taxi—"and then I'll ask if he wants to make an appointment."

It worked, sort of.

She called me back to say that my father had admitted to making up the appointment to get me off his back. I burst into tears. "My father's never lied to me before," I said.

But, she told me, he'd also agreed to come in. At eleven, she

said; she'd let me know what happened. My cell phone rang at
11:15; the doctor had taken Dad's vitals and insisted he go right
across the street to the ER, and Dad had stormed out in a huff,
saying he was fine. I raced over to the ER, arriving to hear him
cursing an orderly. "There's absolutely nothing wrong with me!
I'm only here because of my pain-in-the-ass daughter!"

Blinking back tears, I pulled the curtain aside. My father stared
at me with wild eyes. He'd taken to carrying Mom's cane, and he
stamped it into the floor. "This is absolutely intolerable! Stalin's
Russia has nothing on this place! I'm being held against my will!"

I apologized to the orderly and to the family huddled around
the next bed. When I asked for his keys—"Of course I drove
myself! I'm not incompetent!"—he threw them on the small
metal table. I picked them up.

"Oh, that's just insulting." His voice held withering disdain.

I wheeled around. "I don't care if you feel insulted." My
voice was steely with fury. I'd never spoken to my father in anything resembling the tone I used now, but the man I was speaking
to was not the father I knew. His blue eyes looked childlike, unfamiliar, and oddly blank, as though he didn't know me, either.
"You are in no condition to drive. You might not care about
killing yourself or someone else, but I do. You're in no shape to
decide a thing. I'm leaving."

I went outside the building, dropped to the sidewalk against a
wall, and sobbed. Then I stood up and walked back in. He
grinned as I appeared, reached for my hand. "Hi, honey."

TURNS OUT THE culprit was not a stroke or sudden Alzheimer's—
both of which I'd considered—but what the doctor called danger-

ously low levels of sodium. Once he was pumped through with a few bags of saline solution, Dad was his normal self, flirting with the prettier nurses, ranting against the indignities of hospital food, reading the business pages.

But what had caused the sodium to plummet, and what would keep it from doing so again—as, indeed, it did, the following week?

No one could say. My father went to numerous appointments, grumbling all the way, where specialists ran inconclusive tests. "They're trying to kill me!" he shouted one afternoon on the phone. He referred to the specialists by the street address of the main medical campus, as in, "The gods on Parnassus are trying to kill me!" And then one doctor, a gentle Asian man whom my father liked immediately ("He figured it out!" Dad would say later, getting teary; "the Chinaman figured it out!"), reported that some rare strains of small-cell lung cancer can emit a hormone that depletes the system of sodium.

I had a head cold the day of my father's lobectomy, when the surgeon confirmed that my father had "very bad lung cancer." Maybe that's why I felt an eerie disconnect and considered asking, "Very good lung cancer, what would *that* look like, Doctor?"

This disconnect felt very different from the shock of hearing my mother tell me, five years before, of *her* cancer. Then, I'd written *lungs* and *lymph* and *liver* as if I were transcribing Serbo-Croatian, or Martian. Now, slow tears coursing down my face, it wasn't shock I felt. "You're hardened now," my friend Bonnie said when I described it to her. But it wasn't hardened I felt as much as a trickle of dread, familiar and slow. This time, as with my mother, I felt I'd been tethered to a force beyond my control. I had no choice but to go along, and of course, I wanted to be there for him. The difference was, this time, I knew where it would end. The only surprise left would be how.

MY FATHER BEGAN chemotherapy in March 2005. He experienced momentary relief from the low sodium, and then the levels would fall again, and he'd get irritable, lethargic, weak. "I'm so tired of this roller coaster," he'd say. "I'm really trying to keep up a good attitude, I really am, but I just don't seem to be getting a break."

Dad had never been taciturn with his discomforts; we always knew when he, a lifelong insomniac, had had a bad night because he'd walk around muttering that he'd never sleep again. "This cold," he'd say, after a few days of a runny nose and endless complaints of sinus pressure, "just won't let up." Cancer, of course, was a far cry from a bad cold or a restless sleep. And yet, as much as I tried to buoy my father's spirits and listen patiently to his health fears, I couldn't help but draw unfavorable comparisons to Mom, who during her bout with cancer had never complained. I felt even more acutely Dad's social isolation, as I sat across from him while he picked at his food and said things like, "I don't play bad odds. If this chemo's going to work, it's got to break fifty-fifty." I whipped up soups and whirred Ensure shakes, storing containers in the fridge and then finding them untouched next time I visited. My father had always loved to cook, but now he left the burner on while CNN blared. He continued pouring himself Scotch before dinner, the color of the drink now a pale shade of its once rich amber. But he also drank two or three instead of one.

Once, I offered to get him Ensure instead, and he'd turned a gaze on me like the one I'd seen in the hospital when I picked up his keys. I got the message. Cocktail hour was sacrosanct; and as long as he was alive, he was having a drink, one he'd damn well make himself. One Sunday, parceling out his twelve prescriptions into the weekly dosage box, I discovered that he'd doubled up one day. I worried that I would have to move in. Annie still worked as Dad's housekeeper, and she was a huge help in running to Walgreens at any hour and going to the store. But he didn't want her to cook for him, and when I opened the refrigerator, I often found spoiled vegetables, milkshakes fuzzy with mold.

I gave him inspirational books by Pema Chödrön and talked to him about what I had learned in CBT. I went online and found cancer support groups and Grandparents Raising Grandchildren support groups and widowed people support groups. Notes with names and numbers sat by his phone for weeks. I encouraged him to go to Grace Cathedral, right across the street. One night, I'd even called his therapist, confessing that I felt guilty for doing so but was using the excuse of his being in the hospital. "You need to understand that I will tell him we spoke," she said to me. I made sure I told him first.

I wanted these things to help my father. I wanted him to turn to me one day with sureness in his eyes and say, "I'm going to be fine." He didn't. He let me tuck him into bed and hold his hand and stroke his forehead, but when I closed the door I often heard him weeping. I felt awful then, awful that I couldn't say more to make him feel better, awful that I didn't know what that would be. Often, the reassurances I offered seemed to bounce right off his face as he bowed his head, not making eye contact.

"I know you're right," he'd say, after I'd suggested he call a friend or let me take him out or count his blessings. Lame advice, I knew—but his helplessness brought out the taskmaster in me.

His misery was so laced with self-pity that I felt all of my mother's training rise up in me, against my own better judgment and experience. It hadn't been so long before, after all, that *I'd* been depressed—and the raw fear, however subconscious, of encountering that despair again, even in someone else, made me impatient.

He'd look at me with weary eyes, give a sad sweet smile.

"You're all I have," he said one night. "Everyone else has left me."

"Oh, Daddy," I said.

"I loved Blake so much. No one knows how much I loved that boy. No one loved that boy like I did."

I don't remember how I responded to that. I would have felt a mixture of feelings: compassion, surely, and my own grief, but also a charged and ugly competitiveness, as though Dad and I were in a contest over who loved Blake more. I heard the isolation, too, the implication of his "No one knows." My father felt utterly alone, and standing by his side, I felt unable to convince him differently. I'd like to think I said, "I know, Daddy, I know," but the reality is, I didn't know—not yet, not fully. Later, after he was gone, I would come to understand my father, as I had my mother—in ways not fully available to me when they were alive. But that night, I bent my head, kissed his forehead, reiterated my love, and left the room.

"Turn off the light, would you, honey?"

"Yes, Daddy. Sleep well. I'll call you in the morning."

ONE TUESDAY IN MAY, Dad's first round of chemo complete, we went to see the oncologist. Waiting in the examination room, my dad stepped up to the counter and started doing leg lifts. "I really need to keep up my strength." Just a few months earlier, before the low sodium, Dad had been going to a health club every afternoon to swim and ride the stationary bike; now he could barely get in and out of the car. But I heard a welcome pep in his voice as he counted to ten and then began on the other leg. And then the doctor came in and told him the signs were good: The chemo was working, the tumor had shrunk, the sodium would stabilize. My dad teared up and, as I drove him home, spoke with enthusiasm about attending Dylan's upcoming ninth-grade graduation. And when we ran into a friend on the street outside Dad's building, Dad invited her up for a drink.

She begged off, on her way to a dinner, but I felt heartened. *Dad's himself again.* We chatted in the living room before Dad placed a call to Dylan to discuss a problem that had come up with Dylan's music teacher. It was seven by the time we hung up, and I phoned a nearby restaurant to order takeout. We'd sat down to dinner when the phone rang: Dylan again, troubled and anxious about the teacher, whom he felt close to and whose services Dad had decided to discontinue.

I listened to Dad talk to Dylan, to his steady authoritative tone, his reassurances of love and that he knew what was best, and I felt further encouraged. But Dad, by the time he hung up, was worn out.

He barely ate. "Go on to bed, Daddy," I said. "I'll clean up."

I left about ten, and my father was still up, reading in a chair, a glass of watered-down Scotch at his side.

I phoned the next morning around nine and got voice mail. This seemed odd, because I knew he was expecting a call from Dylan's headmaster. I wondered if he'd taken a sleeping pill. An hour later, I phoned again: still no answer. I'd never known my father to be in bed at ten o'clock in the morning. I wondered if, desperate with insomnia and anxiety, he'd doubled up on the Ambien . . . or had another Scotch. Dread churned in my belly. I told myself he'd probably taken a pill at two or three and turned off the phone ringer, knowing he could return any important calls.

It was almost noon when Annie picked up. "He is sleeping."

"I don't know, Annie," I said. "It's too late."

"You want me to check?"

"Yes, Annie, please."

I heard the phone receiver being placed on the counter and her footsteps as she walked out of the kitchen and then silence as she stepped onto the rug leading into his bedroom. Then footsteps again, this time loud and clattery, and cries. The phone fumbled against the counter as her voice got louder and louder. "Call 911! Call 911! Oh my God! Oh my God!"

I told her to call 911 since she was on the landline, and that I'd be right there. I arrived as the paramedics were angling a stretcher into the elevator. We all went up together and walked in the open door. I pointed to Dad's bedroom, and then I walked into the kitchen, and into the dining room, and into the kitchen again. I went back to the hall and sat on the floor.

My father's oncologist, when I reached him, told me, "This can happen. He may have gotten disoriented, tripped. He might have had a mild stroke. Maybe the tumor has spread to the brain." Huddled paramedics in black coats clustered in the doorway of my father's bedroom, some kneeling to untangle cords and tubes. "They'll take him to the hospital," the oncologist continued. "Let me know as soon as you find out where."

One of the black coats stood up, walked to a box with dials and knobs. I heard a word of medical terminology, an abbreviation that meant nothing. I heard him say "General" into a radio. I called the oncologist back and left the message, but I already knew the problem lay beyond his scope. He must have, too, because he never called back. San Francisco General Hospital is where Blake was taken after he was shot. It has the best trauma unit in the city.

This wasn't a brain tumor.

My father had a large plastic mask over his face when the paramedics wheeled him out. I followed. They loaded the stretcher into the back of the ambulance and when I started to follow, the driver took me aside. "You'll sit up front with me," he said. Another paramedic took off my dad's wristwatch—$9.95 at Walgreens, Dad had proudly announced, a "perfectly decent watch" he'd bought before going into the hospital for his lung surgery so he didn't have to take the gold Omega my mother had given him for their wedding—and told me to hold on to it.

The ambulance pulled away from the curb and headed down the hill. The sirens were very loud, and it took a minute to realize they were coming from right above my head.

At the hospital, I was shown to a series of conference rooms. A social worker introduced herself and sat down. I phoned my friend Linda, my cousin Rick, and Kenneth. They all came. At some point, I called Dylan's school. The switchboard was closed. The voice mail recording said to press a certain number "in case of an emergency."

Rick nodded. "This *is* an emergency, Linds."

I left a message.

Three doctors came in and sat down. The doctors told me

the extent of damage to my father's brain. They told me they did not know, exactly, what had caused it. They told me the cause didn't matter. In cases like this, any percentage of recovery was considered "good," but I needed to know that recovery did not mean cognition. It meant basic motor reflexes, the most rudimentary of brain stem activity. Like a reptile's, I thought, some phrase from my high school biology textbook bubbling up after more than twenty years. The chances of anything approaching "good" were small.

"How small?" I asked. "Single digit?"

The doctors looked at one another. *We can tell her.* Or *We have to tell her.* It happened in an instant, and with uniform assent on their part. Twyla, the doctor I wanted as my friend, spoke. Her blue eyes did not waver. "Less than single digit."

Linda brought water and food. Rick kept his hand on my arm.

I made two decisions. Keep him alive—but no heroic measures, as Dad himself would have put it—until Dylan gets home. Get Dylan home.

What would I tell Dylan? What would I do with Dylan? What was going to happen? What was I going to do?

"You don't have to answer all that now, Linds," Rick said. Linda came in from phoning her parents, her eyes red.

My cell phone rang. The social worker and Linda and Rick nodded at me. *You can do it.*

"Honey," I said, after hearing Dylan's voice, "I'm really sorry I have to tell you this over the phone. I wish I could be there to hold you."

Across the table, Linda and Rick and the social worker nodded again. *You're doing fine. Keep going.*

I did.

Chapter Ten

"But I tell you, look around you, and see how the fields are ripe for harvesting."

Witnessing death, the third time around, does not get any easier. What it does get is more familiar, with an eerie kind of recognition. *Here's the hospital blanket, here's the beep of the heart monitor, there's that smell.* The funneling of time, so an hour feels like five minutes; the attenuation of sensation, so food is only a bland necessity, thirst someone else's idea. Everything outside that bed, that person leaving you forever, falls away.

Dylan flew home immediately, joined by our friends William and Deborah. I met him in front of the hospital as their taxi pulled up, and we went upstairs. Dad had done well during the night, an announcement that had made my hopes soar. But then I understood that doing well, on a brain-trauma ward, is a relative term. I'd signed a DNR that wasn't needed, and the hole they'd drilled in his skull was relieving the pressure. That's what "well" meant.

I asked the nurse to cover the hole with a towel, and I asked Dylan if he wanted to see Grandpa alone or with me. And then, a few hours later, after Rick and my friend Leslie arrived, we all went into a curtained-off corner of the hospital ward with two doctors and the social worker to discuss the next step.

The doctors explained the situation, as they had to me the day before; they'd brought CT scan films. Dylan wanted to see them—he'd just visited a neurology lab on a school field trip for science class, and he asked about parts of the brain I'd never heard of. One of the doctors raised his eyebrow with a kind smile and took Dylan over to the light box.

"I know what my grandpa wanted."

We all looked at Dylan. His face was serene, tear-smudged and puffed, but calm and steady. "My grandpa and I talked about Terri Schiavo." The room itself seemed to suck in its breath.

I'd heard Dad speak of Terri Schiavo, too, by way of the media circus and what asses politicians could be. Dad had never made his opinion on her fate explicit to me. He didn't need to. I'd heard Dad say, anytime we passed what used to be called an old folks' home, "If it gets that bad, just push me off the porch." Since his diagnosis of lung cancer, he'd started filling out a Power of Attorney, in case, as he put it, "I go ga-ga." In the hospital back in January, he'd cleared his throat and told me where the assets were and the name of his accountant and who could help me find an attorney.

"My grandpa told me," Dylan said. "He wouldn't ever want to live like that."

We all breathed out.

"Okay," I said.

"But we don't have to do it today, do we?"

No, of course we didn't.

We did it the next day. Kenneth said Last Rites and sprinkled my father with holy water from Lourdes, brought by Dylan's first friend. Deborah and William said their good-byes and flew back to Connecticut. Sheryl arrived. Dylan had phoned her the night before to tell her what had happened, and she came as soon as she could. There were four of us in the room when my father took a breath and then did not breathe out: Dylan and his mother on one side; Leslie and I on another.

After Dylan and Sheryl left, Leslie and I sat outside on a cement planter. She wrote down the names and numbers of people to call. And then I went back up alone to the small curtained area around my father's bed. For two days, I'd murmured words to my father, raising my voice above a whisper after the nurse drew back the curtain the first night to say, "You know, we don't know that he *can't* hear you." I said them once more, and then I just sat. I picked up the familiar hand, studied its smooth even nails and long fingers, its pink padded palm. It had been my father's hand; I thought of cutting it off so I could take it with me. I watched the sky outside the window, the light on the buildings.

Soon enough, I knew, I'd have to stand up. That wouldn't be hard.

And then I'd have to walk away.

MY DAD HADN'T died the way I'd expected when we got the cancer diagnosis. I'd heard no clear explanation of how he'd fallen, or why, or how long he'd lain there. I couldn't imagine beyond a jumble of confusion, an insult of pain, a panic of terror.

The doctors told me that any cognition—any suffering—would have been brief; the damage was so extensive. But that didn't stop me from wondering. At some point, I gave up. My father had died.

I'd marveled, the afternoon Blake had died, that my parents had known to pick up the Yellow Pages, flip to "Mortuaries," make the call saying where the body could be picked up and that they'd like it to be cremated. Now I picked up the phone, I talked to the mortician and the coroner (city law required an autopsy for head injuries, the hospital had advised me); I delegated the ordering of flowers (no lilies, please) and preprinted sympathy acknowledgment cards. For three days after Dad died, people came to the apartment. My parents' Protestant friends looked nervous, showing up at four o'clock on a Monday, glancing around as though we might break into a séance. "Are you sure? Just dropping in?"

Jewish and Irish friends understood, saying they were glad we were sitting shiva or holding a wake. They brought food, poured drinks, told me to stay seated. I got the most teary at the arrival of my father's oldest friends, men I'd thought of my whole life with "Mr." or "Uncle" in front of their names, men who had been at those cocktail parties that had lasted until midnight, filling our house with cigarette smoke and laughter carrying up the stairs long past bedtime—those men now said nothing but, red-eyed, took me in their arms.

I knew, from having read *The Tibetan Book of Living and Dying* after Blake had died, of the belief that for seven weeks after a body has died, the soul hovers, not yet out of our reach. Through prayer, we can ease the soul's transition to the next world. I prayed every day at 4:18 P.M., the time on the clock when the heart monitor hooked up to my father had hit zero and Dylan, watching it too, had cried out. I knelt on the rug where Dad had lain, now cleaned so you saw the stain only if you knew to look, and pressed my whispered petition into the musty, slightly chemically smelling woolly fibers.

I prayed in church and with Dylan and alone. I didn't say much. My own experience had shown me that the time surrounding death is holy, full of mystery and intensity and intimacy. Finding myself in it again, I leaned back and let it hold me.

The intensity of the first days gave way to a blur of paperwork and duties. I boxed up my dishes and books, and moved out of my apartment and into my father's place. There was so much stuff: cupboards and closets full of my parents' accumulated belongings; papers and files and photos and neatly starched shirts I pressed my face into while gathering them in my arms to take to the secondhand clothing store.

My parents had been married forty years. They moved eight times. They rarely threw anything away. The more important the document, the more copies I found, in various places: wills and trusts; court documents; certificates of birth and death; deeds to houses bought and sold. My hands became covered with paper cuts and abrasions. I sneezed nonstop from the dust.

The cleaning tag on a yellowed christening gown embroidered with lilies of the valley read "February 1967." It hung on a small hanger in a stained, pink quilted bag next to the smocked dresses I'd worn at ages three and four. Going through a stack of Brooks Brothers boxes ("Never throw away a perfectly good box" was one of my mother's rules), I found photos ranging from 1934 (my grandfather, a die-hard Republican who stunned his sons when he later admitted that FDR had saved the country, sitting with other men around a circumspect-looking Herbert Hoover in a lawn chair) to 1973 (an entire roll of my cat's first litter against the backdrop of my pink shag rug). Dad pinning a medal on a soldier, a postcard from a train ride to Chicago in 1940, and—between yellowed clippings from the *New York Times* recipe section—an envelope whose contents were identified in my mother's penciled writing: "Blake's first haircut." And then, of course, the family vacations in the station wagon, the graduations, the holidays.

After ninety minutes on the rug in my father's bedroom going through these boxes, I looked up, exhausted. For a second, I didn't know where I was, I'd been so steeped in a world far too alive to call the past. I looked at the white walls of my father's room, the bed that hadn't been slept in since the night he fell, the boxes of my own books. At the recognition of my own bare feet, the fact that I was the only adult alive to go through those boxes and boxes of unorganized photos and know who was who, I burst into tears.

I'D KNOWN, THE instant I'd picked up the ringing cell phone in that hospital conference room, what it meant. Not just that I had to tell Dylan that Grandpa would die very soon, but that I was in charge now. I had the authority to carry out the responsibility and obligation I'd always felt. Once I knew this, once I *felt* it, there was no question in my mind what I needed to do.

I moved into my father's apartment because it was Dylan's home, and my place was too small for the two of us. Plus, I wanted to keep continuity and security for Dylan. Ever the conscientious attorney, Dad had brought up the inevitable need to make some changes, going so far as to consult me—and a lawyer—about naming me successor guardian. But verbal intentions are not legally binding. I had to file a petition.

Dylan didn't need any convincing. The day before Dad's funeral, Dylan and I went to see friends for dinner. As we sat in their whirlpool and talked about exercise, the horrors of PE class, and this versus that new fitness trend, Dylan turned to me. "Is that going to be your first act as my new guardian, getting me membership at a gym?"

Driving home later, I told him that, yes, I was going through the motions to be appointed his new guardian and that he would live with me.

"That's what my mom wants," he said, and I held my breath. Had I heard right?

And then he clarified: "Mom wants me to live with her."

I spoke carefully, neutrally. "What do you want?"

He stared out the window.

"Listen, Dyl. Don't worry about hurting my feelings. Tell me the truth. Either way, I need to know."

"I don't want to have to say."

"Okay. We can talk about it later."

"No, I don't want to have to say in court. I don't want to have to choose in front of my mom. I want to live with you."

"You won't have to stand up in court. You won't be put on the spot."

My father's colleagues, many of them also longtime family friends, had rallied around me with advice, support, and recommendations, and I soon had an attorney. He reassured me of Dylan's role in the guardianship process. At fifteen, Dylan had much say in the outcome; the court would weigh his wishes. More than mine, and—in this case, given the precedent of fourteen years—more than his mother's. Dylan's views would be made known before the court date through the report of a court-appointed investigator, and if

Dylan wanted to add anything, an attorney could approach the judge and ask for privacy.

In the weeks after Dad's death, Sheryl had phoned to ask me when it would be all right to see Dylan. She had sat next to me at Dad's funeral. I was glad to have her there—just as I'd welcomed her presence in the hospital. We were family, after all. She'd been consistently reliable for years. Dad had often expressed to me his respect for how she'd "pulled her life together," taking classes and teaching herself computer skills. She and her mother had flown back east to attend Dylan's ninth-grade graduation. On the phone one afternoon, she told me that she was fine with Dylan's living with me and his continuing as a boarder, as he'd chosen to do, for high school. But she didn't think he needed a guardian. "I'm his mother," she told me. "It's time I got to make the decisions."

"Okay. . . . What kind of decisions?"

"You know," she said. "Decisions." Her voice trembled. "I've never been allowed to be a mother to him, Lindsey!"

A few days later, she sent me a Web link describing the duties of conservators and appointed caretakers. "Don't caretakers go home at the end of their shift?" I asked my attorney. "And what kind of benefits and salary should I ask for?"

Sarcasm aside, I couldn't see any way to reconcile his living with me and her making decisions, and the more I tried to explain why, the more entrenched she and I became in our positions.

For years, we'd said little to each other beyond "Hi," "How are you?" and "Take care." There had always been a stiltedness between us, a tension around all that wasn't said. She'd married my drug-addicted brother and given birth to a boy my parents had reared during their retirement and illnesses. I was the sister of a man she'd loved and lost, a woman who'd spent more time with her son than she had.

Now, she said I was trying to steal Dylan. "Of course he'll pick you!" she shouted. "You spoil him rotten." I'd started to reply—"Actually, I don't"—when she interrupted that she'd never even been allowed to see Blake on his deathbed. That's when I snapped.

"I wouldn't bring up the past if I were you," I told her. "I can go there, too." And when she said that she hadn't been allowed to see Dylan all summer, I held out the phone, flabbergasted. "He's been right here!" I shouted. "You could have seen him anytime. You never asked."

"That's the point, Lindsey! I shouldn't have to ask."

"Anytime in fifteen years, you could've stepped up to the plate and been a mother to him. Anytime. You never have. That's not my fault."

All I heard then was dial tone, because she'd hung up. But in my fury I'd spoken what, to me, was the crux of the issue.

I didn't speak to her for the rest of the summer.

"You're just weak," Dylan announced one evening, after he brought me the phone with her on the other end and I shook my head. "You're just letting your emotions get in the way."

Dylan had grown by then so that he stood only an inch shorter than I. I put down the dish towel I was holding and walked over to him, stood with my face right up against his. My voice was low and steady and firm. "I'm really sorry you're caught in the middle. I know how awful this is for you. And you're right. I am emotional. This is a very emotional situation. You can't let yourself feel it right now, but it's there. I saw your daddy—and your mom—do things that made me really angry. I have a really hard time dealing with people who don't take responsibility for their behavior. I think you know that about me. But don't call it weakness because, frankly, you don't know what you're talking about. There's no reason you would. It's just a fact."

The rest of that evening, he wouldn't leave my side.

The truth was, not only did I see no point in talking further with Dylan's mom—we'd each made our case; there was no more to say—but I was scared to. I've never been good at confrontation, and I'm much too willing to take responsibility for someone else's pain. Raw from the loss of my dad—if running on adrenaline from the duties that pulled at me—I had to protect myself. And yet, as much as I'd wrestled with my duty toward Dylan in the past, I had no qualms now. This wasn't about winning Dylan in a contest or stealing him; this was about doing what I felt I had to.

One evening, my friend Eve came over. A musician, she had asked me to help her write lyrics for a song about *metta,* the Buddhist concept of lovingkindness to which she'd introduced me a few years earlier. As we worked on the phrases, I thought of Sheryl. I couldn't pretend to know the complexity of her feelings, but writing the song with Eve helped me to see that she hurt, too, and that she wanted the same things I did. Love. Compassion. What was best for her son. She and I might not agree, but we were in a relationship. And prayer had shown me that you don't honor a relationship by running from it.

As the court date approached, Dylan and I spent most nights sitting up late talking. He asked why he'd moved in with Grandma and Grandpa in the first place. I told the story he'd heard many times before, but this time I went deeper. I answered questions he'd never before asked. I explained drug addiction and why it wasn't merely, as he put it, "stupid." I repeated that his parents loved him very much but had been unfit to care for him properly. That wasn't his fault. Blake, I told him, had died with great sorrow that he'd let Dylan down. His father, I told him, was wonderful and generous and the funniest person I'd ever known, but also devastated by drugs.

Dylan has always been self-possessed, at times uncannily so. At fifteen, he'd had more loss than many fifty-year-olds. His grandpa had been gone only three months, and he was the object of a custody battle.

"I have only one question," he said, turning to me his steady blue eyes, his placid and determined face, his set jaw. I felt the enormity of the moment, and the inevitability of it. Here was the boy I'd held that Thanksgiving in 1990, when we'd stared at each other: *You*. In the years since, there had been the silly jokes, the confidences, the Christmas afternoon he'd found his pet mouse dead in her cage. We were due at my cousin's in an hour, and Mom reminded me that Dylan needed to put on a clean shirt. "Go ahead," I told her and Dad. "We'll follow later. We've got something more important to do." I picked up the cage and some paper towels and a trowel, and told Dylan to find a nice spot in the garden. There were many such moments, moments I'd been there for him, moments he'd filled my life with purpose—and somehow, in the fullness of time, they'd not only led to this but held this in them all along.

"What's that?"

"Why do people have babies if they can't take care of them? I wouldn't get a dog if I couldn't take care of it."

The night before the guardianship hearing, I showed Dylan a letter I'd written in 1996, on what would have been Blake's twenty-ninth birthday. In it, I described the brother I adored, the man I wanted Dylan to know, if only on paper, to balance out the victim of a drug deal gone bad. The letter is three pages, front and back, and I watched Dylan place each sheet on his lap as he finished. I watched his face move from stoic absorption to a slight frown and then a crumpled sob as he cried the first tears I'd heard him cry over his father in more than ten years. "I wish I'd known him."

THE NEXT DAY was bright and sunny, summer already sliding into fall, often the warmest season in San Francisco. The only suit I have is blue wool, but I wore it with a linen blouse and bare legs. It had been my mother's suit, and I'd had it altered a few years earlier—too much, it turned out, because as I sat, ramrod straight, the waistband cinched. I'd asked my friend Leslie and my cousin Rick to come to court, and they sat in the gallery, as did Sheryl's mother, who'd come with her boyfriend, and Sheryl.

We all watched a movie about the legal responsibilities of guardianship. The judge walked in, and we all stood. We were called forward. My attorney spoke, reiterating the position of the petition; Dylan's court-appointed attorney spoke, presenting her advocacy of Dylan; the judge nodded. I stared straight ahead. Sheryl spoke, repeating in essence what she'd told me: Dylan didn't need a legal guardian, since he was at school nine months of the year. He was almost an adult, and he could live with me, but she—his mother—wanted to make some decisions.

There was a pause.

Should I say anything? I wrote on a notepad. My lawyer wrote, *Nope.* The judge, poker-faced, listened.

And then Dylan stood up. In the past few weeks, Dylan had

changed his mind about speaking in court. He'd announced, after the court-appointed investigator had visited us, that he wanted to speak for himself.

"You don't have to," I reminded him.

"I want to," he said.

"Okay, but remember that you can change your mind, even at the last minute. You don't have to say anything."

"I know."

I didn't watch him as he spoke, but I have a visual memory of him standing in a blue suit with one of my father's ties and in a pair of Dad's shoes. His posture was straight, his hair neatly combed. He spoke clearly. "I think that the person who takes care of me should be the person who gets to make the decisions. If my mother doesn't want to take care of me, she shouldn't get to make the decisions. I think Lindsey should be my guardian."

The judge nodded, not in visible agreement as much as acknowledgment that she'd heard. Dylan sat down. And the judge spoke her decision.

OFFICIAL LETTERS OF guardianship, stamped and signed, went into a file for anyone who needed proof. The real assurance, I already had. I took Dylan to high school, and then I took myself to the Big Island, where for a week my biggest decision involved whether to sit in a chaise or lie on the hammock. Sheryl and I made plans for the holidays, and we spoke with a new comfort. My role was clarified, and I wanted her to spend as much time with Dylan as she could.

In February, six months after the hearing, I flew to New York to see Dylan. We'd arranged to meet near Grand Central, and I had the cab swing by on my way from the airport. Dylan waved from the doorway of the Cornell Club, where he was waiting with friends, and got in the backseat, bending over to rummage in his backpack for a book.

"Sweetie! Hi!" I pulled his head toward me, kissed his smelly hair. "Look at me!"

"I want to find my book," he said, head still bowed. "I want to show it to you."

"You haven't seen me in six weeks!" I rumpled his hair. "I want to look at you."

He squirmed. "I want to find my book."

"But I'm right here."

"Exactly." Bent forward, digging around through CDs and papers and gum wrappers and an empty water bottle, he didn't look up. "You'll always be right here."

A few years ago, swimming laps at Spieker Pool on the UC Berkeley campus, I thought about the college student I'd been, some twenty years earlier. Daydreamy and hesitant, I'd been interested in writing but too shy to try out for the school paper or go to office hours. I'd never swam in any of the three outdoor, gorgeous pools on campus. Neither activity had occurred to me back then, although I'd always loved writing and swimming.

And here I was moving back and forth in Spieker Pool in 2003, unable to imagine life without writing or swimming. I knew I couldn't go back to 1981—any more than I could go back to a night in 1992 when a drummer I'd met at a party in New York invited me to hear his band play at the Bottom Line and I said no thanks, because the gig didn't start until ten and I had to work the next day. If he was so interested, I told my journal (and my brother; this happened around the time Blake and I had reconnected at Thanksgiving when he was in treatment), Paul would ask me out again. (Even Blake, recovering drug addict that he was, saw what I couldn't: "Oh, hon," he said, shaking his head, "that's not the way it's done.")

Opportunity, I told myself as I held my own in the Medium Fast lane. *You can't go back, but you can seize it now.*

It had taken me a while to figure out, but I'd be a fool not to listen. So, the autumn after my dad died, when a man Dylan had befriended at Grace Cathedral invited us to an event there, I went. As I sat in the pew after the choir finished with Evensong and the altar party filed out, I thought, *Don't get up.* Sitting in the quiet, vaulting space, I felt something I hadn't even realized I'd thirsted for.

Someone sneezed. Another person cleared her throat. The woman in front of me shifted her weight to adjust a shawl around her shoulders. A man breathed from the back of his throat, as though he might have fallen asleep. These sounds weren't off-putting or distracting. Instead, they felt supportive and affirming. The calm and quiet in silence around others differs from that of silence alone. The chapel held an intimacy in the noises, the shared air, the bodies breathing. *Yes,* the presence of other people says. *Keep going. We're in this together.*

Silence isn't empty at all.

You are here, I am here. The permission I'd first felt in prayer had changed my life. And when I came across a translation of the Fourth Psalm that read, *"Bring your gifts, just as you are,"* I knew the absolute love of being worthy, just by being there. Now, sitting in Grace Cathedral and wanting to stay there all evening and into the night, I felt that permission—indeed, that invitation—again. This time I was being pushed to pray in the company of others. Not just every Sunday, but in a new way I didn't know yet. But I understood enough to listen, and respond.

The first thing I noticed, a few weeks later when I showed up at St. Gregory of Nyssa Episcopal Church, was the light: faint and watery, creeping in through the windows where paperwhites bloomed on the sill. I'd arrived for a Centering Prayer group that meets every Friday at 7:20 A.M. in Potrero Hill. To get there meant leaving the house at 6:40. It meant getting up at six, and dressing, and having a little something to eat as well as a cup of coffee. It meant a disruption in my routine. The resistance had welled up as soon as I'd slapped off the alarm. Why was I getting up again?

I reminded myself of the impulse, the desire that had felt like a calling. I went.

The next thing that struck me, that first Friday, after a man who introduced himself as Mark rang the bell and we all went quiet, was the sensation of plummeting, straight down, without fear. Fast. Slippery. Welcome. Just as I'd sensed in those moments in Grace Cathedral, praying in community allows a focus and depth that, at home, feels more evasive. At home, I'm more likely to be distracted by a mosquito bite or the view in front of me. *The windows really do need washing. I'd better stop at Trader Joe's for more seltzer water.* But when I'm sitting with other people, letting go happens more effortlessly. Maybe it *is* a kind of peer pressure, but it works. And when it works, I lose awareness of it. I don't watch the woman across from me to see if her posture is better than mine. I don't spy on Mark to see if he really isn't moving, or if it just seems that way. I can fall into deep contemplative space at home alone, of course; and I often have. But it's the transition *into* prayer that's tricky for me. Letting go of the details can be liberating, but also anxiety producing. If I strip them away, what will be there? Just me, naked in the middle of Bayview Avenue.

I'd been going to St. Gregory's for three weeks when, one Friday, something loomed on the periphery. It wasn't close enough to identify, or even to make out its shape, but I knew what it held. I focused on my breath, on the image of surf: *In. Out.* I kept my eyes closed and my feet on the floor and my hands in my lap. *There it is: the scary place.*

When I was back in my car, I thought how familiar and vivid the scariness had seemed, like those occasional dreams where I'm depressed again, the despair so palpable that, during the dream, there's no way out. By then, though, as I turned the key in the ignition and watched the freeway traffic glisten silver against the pinkening just-before-eight-A.M. sky, I felt some distance, some perspective. It wouldn't be fair, or accurate, to say that the distance held any guarantee. But it was sufficient for me to think, *Well, okay then. There it is.* And as I drove away, I reminded myself I'd be back the following Friday at 7:20.

We are one in the body of Christ.

Phrases like that used to confound me. Now, when being in community holds me like a trapeze harness for sailing out over the void, I get it.

I STAYED IN my father's apartment another seven months after the guardianship hearing. We hosted Thanksgiving and Christmas

Eve, and then Dylan went back for spring term. And, in January, on what would have been my brother's thirty-ninth birthday, I walked into the physical manifestation of a floor plan I'd seen in my mind's eye for years: the typical layout of a San Francisco Edwardian flat. During my real estate search, of course, I'd seen many of them, but they all had only two bedrooms. "You can use the dining room as an office," Realtors would offer up with sunny smiles, and I'd keep looking.

This one had a master bedroom, a room for Dylan, *and* an office. And the dining room—at the other end of the hall—had room enough for my parents' old farm table. It also had a view of the Golden Gate Bridge, not just the north tower but the whole thing. Add to that the coincidence that the Realtor showing the place had been my brother's high school French teacher, and all of it seemed ordained.

In April, I moved in after a flurry of painting and smashing through closets made from corrugated cardboard, after culling three generations of accumulated furniture and books. And after the movers and the guys from the hospice charity and 1-800-GOT-JUNK came and took everything, I returned to my father's apartment. I knelt on the floor where the paramedics had huddled. The carpet had been pulled up, so I knelt on the remaining mat. I had kept a sprig of dried grasses from the previous October, when I'd gone up to Mount Tam, and I carried it now to the fireplace. I pulled aside the metal link curtain. I flicked one of my father's old cheap Bic lighters. The grass caught, not in a surge of flame but in the gradual outlining of stem and leaf with a rim of black. I closed my eyes. I watched the grass burn.

"You can go now, Daddy," I said.

And then, so could I.

IN THE MORNING, as soon as I get up, I make coffee. Then I find the place. Some days it's a cushion on the floor, others it's one of the straight-backed dining room chairs. Lately I've been sitting with my back to the window in a chair I never particularly liked but that feels perfect for this. I've considered using the prayer rug for its intended purpose; I've already got it properly oriented, but I like having it at the top of the stairs and that feels too exposed to the street because of the window below. On Fridays, I'm off to St. Gregory's for Centering Prayer; every Sunday, to mass.

Loss forms us, yes, and loss, you could say, brought me to prayer. But it's love that keeps me coming back.

Epilogue

The watery light of winter has made way for full summer sunshine at 7:15 A.M. I pull up to the curb outside St. Gregory's and park the car. Across the street, eighteen-wheelers maneuver and beep their way out of the Anchor Steam Brewery loading docks. I walk into the sanctuary, pausing for my eyes to adjust to the dim of the vestibule, and choose my seat. Smiling a greeting at Mark and Cathleen and whoever else has shown up, early on a Friday morning, for Centering Prayer at this church on the corner of Mariposa and DeHaro on Potrero Hill, I put down my bag, take off my glasses, close my eyes, take a deep breath. Mark rings the bell and I slide down the hole into a sensation so expansive that it seems a physical place, a place that can't be conjured but that always greets me with welcome familiarity.

My chest rises and lowers. *Breathe from your belly,* I've been told in yoga and on the massage table, but to focus on my belly would mean losing the whole. I stay in the sensation, for I don't know how long.

Words come to me, phrases bubbling up. They're perfect. They hold the purpose of language, the promise of connection.

I'd like to grab each one with a net and scoop it onto the shore where it will wait for me. I have every intention of tossing it back when I'm done. How inconvenient, to get a flash of insight when I can't write it down!

In, out, breathe.

Across from me, Mark sneezes. The sun on my shoulders is warm, like my childhood cat who used to drape herself there when I sat in a green corduroy chair to read.

What was that word again? *In, out, breathe. You are praying now, not writing. Breathe.*

It'll come back. Won't it? But the more I watch for it, the more it disintegrates, like individual noodles on the surface of alphabet soup. They don't add up to anything I can read. A Greek sigma, an upper case A with a Norwegian halo, a tilde riding the crest of an N. Symbols; they are just symbols. They articulate the experience, but they are not the experience.

Later, in the car, I'll rummage under the seat for a scrap of paper and write down *alphabet soup.* That'll be enough, back at my desk, to jog my memory. But now I'm in the moment I'll later try to describe. *So be in it.*

I let my fingers forget that they know how to write, that they've ever held a pencil. In my lap, the nest of bones and ligament and skin that makes up my clasped hands gives off a radiating static, a consciousness. If I had to, I could isolate the middle knuckle, say, of my left pinky. But I don't have to. My body is a shell, and my breath moves through it, the way Tassajara Creek moves through the mountains.

When Mark taps the bowl, the sound is faint. I hear it the way I once saw the tops of oak trees through the Morrisons' overheated pool when I swam underwater in it as a child. Up there, out there, and I'm still in here. My chest expands, sinks back.

Was that the bell again, or just the awareness that I heard it the first time? Either way, I heard it. My eyes open, as though the lifting of my eyelids were part of the breath. In front of me on the carpet, I see a two-dimensional figure, a shadow. It has prominent ears, sloping shoulders, and a smooth head. When I was fourteen and on vacation on Maui with my family, I saw a lifesize Mylar cutout of Jesus in the window of a small chapel near Charles Lindbergh's grave. It stopped me cold: I thought I was seeing the risen Christ in the flesh. This shadow on the carpet doesn't make me gasp, the way that Mylar cutout had. But it does seem Other, portentous with Message. It looks like a statue of the Buddha. Still, calm.

Mark taps the bowl again, and its sound ripples outward like water broken by a tossed pebble. I hear the voices outside the pool, my mother calling my name as I come up for a big gulp before going back down so fast that, later, I can say I didn't hear her. I swim the whole length of the Morrisons' pool underwater, feet frog-kicking, lungs burning. And then, up, up toward the sky and the wavering oak branches, up toward my mother's face, up toward the air.

The bell, again. I'm closer and closer, the surface right there. My hand breaks through before my head, so that for one last second, one last moment of suspension, I'm still weightless and free.

And then I'm out. I shake the water from my face and gulp air. I lean forward in the chair and reach my hands to my ankles, pull. The sun warms my entire back as I stretch, and the shadow on the carpet moves. Hair pulled back, body unmoving, that calm was me.

ACKNOWLEDGMENTS

During the writing of this book, many people have stepped forward with generosity, wisdom, critical insight, and friendship.

I am enormously grateful to Michael Frank and Rachel Howard—

To Leslie Dreyfous McCarthy—

To Louise Aronson, Natalie Baszile, Adrianne Bee, Susan Coss, Anne Marino, Stephanie Rapp, Ken Samuels, and Frances Stroh—

To Carol Mann and Will Sherlin; to Shaye Areheart, Anne Berry, Josh Poole, Amy Boorstein, Mark McCauslin, Laura Duffy, Lauren Dong, Sarah Chance Breivogel, Kira Stevens, and the Harmony team; to Paolo Pepe—

To Alice Gordon, Barbara Jones, Sheryl Fullerton, Gregory Wolfe, Mary Kenagy, C. Michael Curtis, Phil Zaleski, Brenda Miller, Lorna Knowles Blake, and Paul Elie—

To Eva Bovenzi, Eve Decker, the Reverend Mary Moore Gaines, Jim Gunshinan, Mark Lodico, David Robertson, and Alan Williamson—

To Sheila Pleasants, Suny Monk, and the staff at Virginia Center for the Creative Arts; to Susan Page Tillett, Susan Hoagland, and the staff at Ragdale; to the people at the Mechanics Institute in San Francisco and the Rose Reading Room at the

New York Public Library; to the SF Writers' Grotto, especially Melanie Gideon and Po Bronson—

To the communities of All Saints' Episcopal Church, Grace Cathedral, and St. Gregory of Nyssa Episcopal Church (all in San Francisco), the Bishop's Ranch in Healdsburg, California, and the Tassajara Zen Mountain Center in the Ventana Wilderness. Special thanks to the Reverend Kenneth L. Schmidt, the Reverend Pamela L. Cranston, and the Reverend Amelia Hagen—

To Judith Pearson, Raya Abraham, Bev Lehr, and Dr. B.—

To Kim Church, Bonnie Grossman, Amy Mezey, Murrey Nelson, Linda Nusser, Joan Svoboda, Erie Vitiello—

To Rick Blake—

To Sheryl—

To Dylan—

YOU ARE THE world to me, and the kingdom of heaven, too.